NAPA WINE COUNTRY

NAPA WINE COUNTRY

REVISED AND EXPANDED

PHOTOGRAPHY AND WORDS
BY EARL ROBERGE

International Standard Book Number 0-912856-97-1
Library of Congress Catalog Card Number 75-16054
Copyright © 1975, 1985 by Graphic Arts Center Publishing Company
P.O. Box 10306, Portland, Oregon 97210 • 503/226-2402
Editor-in-Chief • Douglas A. Pfeiffer
Designer • Robert Reynolds
Typographer • Paul O. Giesey/Adcrafters
Printer • Graphic Arts Center
Bindery • Lincoln & Allen
Printed in the United States of America
First Edition: 1975
Second Edition: 1985

To Joe Heitz, superb winemaker,
gracious and generous host,
secret intellectual, good friend,
and to Alice, his good right arm,
this book is affectionately dedicated.

CONTENTS

"This is the story

of a place   ix

. . . . . . its people.

. . . . . . its product

. . . . . . its way

of life.

A land created on a day

when God was smiling......   xv

. . . . . . and it is called

the Napa Valley.

ACKNOWLEDGEMENTS

How do you say "Thank You" to a whole valley in a manner that does justice to services rendered? That is the problem facing me now, for good manners, as well as simple justice, require that proper credit be given to the many, many people who have lent me a helping hand along the way; they made the telling of the Napa Valley story not only possible, but also a very pleasurable, very warm human experience.

The temptation to emulate Alexander the Great and cut the Gordian knot with a few blanket "Thank You" paragraphs is there, of course, but will be denied. Instead, I must try to unravel the chain of events that led to this book.

If the dream is father of the thought, as the thought is father of the deed, then this book dates back to 1970 and the quaint little wine town of Zell in Germany. In the company of the eminent German writer A. E. Johann, I was sitting in the main room of the Schloss Zell, a 500-year-old castle, that was once the summer home of an emperor of the Holy Roman Empire. We were appreciatively sipping a very exceptional 37-year-old Mosel wine that was perfumed, liquid sunshine. The enjoyment of that wine was much enhanced by sharing it with A. E. who, as well as being Germany's foremost travel writer, is also a renowned gourmet with a fantastic knowledge of fine foods and wines, not only of his native Germany, but also of all parts of the world where he has traveled... and he's been everywhere.

The enjoyment of that superb wine was such that I idly remarked that the whole world should be told about the Mosel region and the wines produced there. A. E.'s reply was "Rather, tell the world about the wonderful wines produced in your own country. The whole world knows about Bordeaux, Burgundy and the Mosel; but California is the Cinderella of the wine world."

Coming from a man who knows wine the way this urbane citizen of the world does, that's quite an endorsement. Of course, I had for years enjoyed California wines, especially those of the Napa Valley, since it seemed that the majority of the wines I liked came from that region. I had, however, never seen the Valley.

It is a simple truism that the best subject for a story is one about which one has some knowledge, and which is of general interest. The wines of California were, therefore, a natural subject for me, since I have been an appreciator and taster of good wines for some thirty years; and interest in the wines California produces was at an all-time peak. So, combining business with pleasure, for our twenty-eighth wedding anniversary trip, my wife and I turned the nose of our red XKE Jaguar toward San Francisco and the California wine country. It was love at first sight.

The 1973 harvest had just about been completed, and the Valley was a colorful patchwork of scarlet and gold — as enticing a photographic subject as I have ever seen. In the back of my mind was the idea that if the 1974 vintage should prove to be a smaller one, I could always use some pictures from 1973, which was already being hailed as one of the best years the Valley had ever experienced; and indeed several pictures from that particular trip are included in this book.

Right from the beginning I received samples of the famed Napa Valley hospitality. At Sterling Vineyards, my first stop, Larry Snideman and Bruce Macumber made me welcome, showed me their spectacular winery, and firmly planted in my mind the idea that in starting with the Napa Valley I was skimming the cream. John Michels of Oakville Vineyards not only took time from a busy day to show me where the last of the Valley's Cabernet Sauvignon grapes were being harvested, but also graciously took me up into the mountains to show me Mont La Salle and Bob Travers's mountainous Mayacamas Vineyards. My thanks go to these people, as well as to Brother Cormack, F.S.C., who was my guide to the far reaches of Mont La Salle's mountain vineyards on an autumn day that I shall always remember as one of transcendental beauty. We left the Valley with the idea that if all the California wine country were as beautiful as this, the book undoubtedly would be a labor of love.

In order that I might see the wine country in all phases of the year, my next trip was in February 1974. Since I still had the idea that this book should be on the wines of California, I spent a day or so with John and George Parducci at their winery in Ukiah. Also, I met August Sebastiani at Sonoma and savored some of the fabulous hospitality for which these people are famous. Subsequent events led to the conclusion that this book should be on the Napa Valley alone, but it is always with a pang of regret that I remember these helpful, knowledgeable and hospitable people whose acquaintance I treasure. Meeting and working with people like these proves to me that the California wine country breeds a special kind of people who are almost invariably courteous, hardworking and helpful.

Somewhere along the line — I believe it must have been during the course of my third trip, in April — it began to dawn on me that a definitive book on California wines would be a tome a foot thick, so expensive no one could afford it.

I shall always be grateful to Mike Robbins, not only because of the courtesies he showed me at his Spring Mountain winery, but also because he introduced me to Joe and Alice Heitz. By this time I was meeting Valley people every day, but the process notably accelerated once I got to know Joe and Alice. Around that table, I met people who have especially influenced the wine scene in California, and who were, without exception, informative, intelligent and extremely knowledgeable on wines, as well as on practically any other subject that happened to be under discussion.

The Napa Valley is a region of supreme chauvinists, but has no booster more perfervid than that human dynamo, Bob Mondavi. In the course of a wonderful evening, made memorable by the company of his delightful family and enhanced by generous libations of the world's finest wines, this talented, persuasive charmer put my foot on the first rung of the ladder that would reach to the stars... or so he convinced me. Few people can resist Bob Mondavi when he decides to sell something—and here he was selling an idea that had been close to his heart for thirty years: that the Napa Valley can, and does, produce the world's finest wines, and someone should tell the world about it. Since he was speaking directly to me alone, I rather got the point.

The "Heitz Hilton," Joe Heitz's delightful guest house, was my refuge for many nights. On this evening Joe was waiting for me with more good wine and the studied logic which is his long point. This quiet, extremely

Left: Chateau Chevalier, on Spring Mountain.

intelligent man has a mind that works as responsively as a well-tuned violin, and he played "molto con expressione" on my already receptive mind. What Bob started, Joe finished; and by 4:00 A.M. I was convinced of the need to focus the book on the Napa Valley so I could adequately cover all the facets of this premium wine region.

Looking back at that evening, I can truly say that the only experience akin to it is getting married. Once you've taken the plunge, you find out the water's fine, and if a bit over your head, easily negotiated by learning to swim. I've never regretted either decision.

The trend of events gets a bit blurred after the third, fourth and fifth trips to the Valley, but certain people and events stand out simply because they helped so much it would be unjust not to mention them.

I remember a beautiful Saturday morning in February when Michael Mondavi used his day off to show me the prettiest parts of the Napa Valley, including the Carmelite Monastery which is one of my favorite retreats, and an old, abandoned winery that would make the world's finest V.I.P. lounge and tasting room. This intense, straight-thinking young man is a worthy successor to his dynamic father and a delightful companion for a day's outing in the Valley. My thanks to him for having provided me one of my most beautiful days.

Another "Thank You" for contributions over and above the call of duty goes to Pat Amick who got up at 5:00 A.M. to fire five smudgepots so I could see what the Valley looks like on a frosty night—and triggered off every wind machine in two miles! This book is truly a Valley project: without help like this, it never would have been possible.

The crush is the heart of the whole wine cycle, and though I had almost three months to do that part of the work, my time was utilized most effectively when Paula Galleron, the daughter of a prominent grower family, was my volunteer guide over the network of back roads that lead to some of the most interesting and picturesque parts of the Valley. Paula was born in these parts, knows everyone, and immeasurably aided my work; for no door was ever closed to this vivacious daughter of the Valley. She also showed me my first view of the Valley from the air, for this talented young lady is also an accomplished pilot; and parts of the Napa Valley are best seen from a plane. Paula's interest in photography, her artistic appreciation and her invariable good nature made her not only a wonderful helper, but a delightful companion. I can only try to adequately express my thanks to her and to her wonderful, hospitable family.

Some aerial pictures can best be made from a helicopter. Laurie Wood knows that, so he and Chuck Carpy arranged for some free helicopter time. Now, that's a real favor; for I've hired helicopters before, and I know how much their kind efforts saved me. My thanks to both of these gentlemen. May their vineyards come down with botrytis every year!

I have already mentioned the large role the Robert Mondavi family had in my stay in the Valley. Suffice it to say that I found in Bob Mondavi a kindred soul who enjoys work as thoroughly as he enjoys play. To Bob, my sometimes tennis partner and often opponent, my sincere thanks for making me feel at home in this Valley. To Marge Mondavi, who has always been so pleasant to me, my sincere respect and affection.

Anyone who has ever been in this Valley for more than twenty-four hours hears about Hanns Kornell, usually described as a crusty old German with a heart of pure mush. He lives up to the description, but it is a shame the whole world doesn't know this man and draw inspiration from him. To Hanns, Marilouise, Paula and Peter, my deep appreciation for so often taking me into their family circle and making me feel one with it. Then, too, who could ever forget that lovely dinner at the Hanns Kornell ranch? There over a hundred people were entertained effortlessly and gracefully by a host and hostess to whom a tour de force like this seems to come easily.

Another person who is a Valley tradition and who far surpassed his billing is Brother Timothy, F.S.C., the famed cellarmaster of The Christian Brothers. Brother Tim is best described as "kindly"... though not necessarily by those who compete with him. This gentle, gracious man has been, from our very first meeting, cooperative, helpful and a mine of useful, pertinent information. There is much of Brother Tim in this book; and if it has any merit, some of the credit can be traced back to this generous man who so well epitomizes all that is best in the Napa Valley. My thanks also go to Brothers Frederick, James, Thomas, and Cormack, each of whom helped to make my stay in the Valley not only pleasant but also very productive.

Jack and Jamie Davies have many friends and admirers, but none more devoted than I. During my stay in the Valley, I have feasted at their table, been a guest at their crush party, shared in their picnics and tasted some very sophisticated champagne. Jack, with his learned approach to wine making, was a font of pertinent information; while Jamie, my regular tennis partner and opponent, helped me keep my waistline within reasonable limits. They make a completely charming family whom I am honored to list with my very good friends. Among friends many things are known instinctively, so I know they will realize the depth of my gratitude.

Many people know Bob and Patsy Wood, for these two are representative of the really "beautiful people" I met in the Napa Valley. When they heard I needed a place to stay, their pool-house was offered—and gratefully accepted, so I had a completely satisfactory place where I could live, work and, on one memorable occasion, entertain. Bob grows some of the best grapes in the Napa Valley; and Patsy, besides being a fabulous cook and indefatigable gardener, is one of those delightful human beings who always makes you feel glad just be around her—a wonderful, fun couple whom I can't possibly thank enough. This is one of the bonuses my stay in the Valley has produced. Bob and Patsy will hopefully be my friends for life.

A stay of several months with a dinner invitation almost every night would produce a very long list of "Thank You's," so here I must hedge a bit and start expressing my appreciation in general, rather than specifically. There are highlights, of course: the baronial splendor and easy warmth of Elizabeth and Louis Martini's beautiful home; the wonderful banter and good food around Greg and Julie Moretton's table; the easy informality, good food and fine wine found at the Tom Lynch and Bill Stafford homes; and the candlelit elegance of Ron and Pat Amick's lovely Rutherford dining room. My thanks also go to Peter Mondavi, for his gracious hospitality. My special thanks also go to Johnsye Dietz Elliot who dresses up any table with superlative music, conversation and cookery.

Many of the outstanding vintners in the Napa Valley got their start somewhere else. Donn and Molly Chapellet are people who left a socialite existence in Beverly Hills for the much more rewarding experience of living on Pritchard Hill and making good wine. To Donn, Molly and all the children, my thanks for having taken me into your family circle and making me feel at home. The several times I have sat at your table and taken in some of the best the Napa Valley can afford—whether it be food, wine, conversation, scenery or beauty—rank as some of the most enjoyable events in a year studded with memorable moments.

The Napa Valley has often been accused of not sufficiently tooting its own horn, but I met a few people who do a pretty good job of telling the world about what a wonderful place it is. Margot Venezia of Oakville Vineyards, Bob Pecota of Beringer Brothers, Joe Maganini of Charles Krug, Maynard Moynihan of Beaulieu, Jerry Gleeson of The Christian Brothers, and Brady McManus of Inglenook—all are competent people who have my admiration for the work they do, and my thanks for the help they have given me.

Then, there's Margrit Biever. Margrit is one of those phenomena occurring only too seldom. Long before I had the pleasure of meeting her, I had heard of Margrit and found myself wondering whether it could possibly be true that one woman could conduct V.I.P. tours in eight languages, arrange a concert, translate technical letters into four languages, cook a superb dinner for thirty people, run a very efficient public relations department, and be at all times one of the most consummate charmers anyone could ever observe—and all in the course of one day's work! She can, and does, do all these things, and with a flair that makes her the envy of anyone who tries to emulate her. She also plays a smashing game of tennis and is at all times a completely delightful person to know. My thanks, admiration, and affection go to her for the unstinted help she has given me in putting together this book. It just wouldn't have been nearly as much fun without her. My thanks also go to Julie Patterson, Margrit's efficient secretary, who makes any day wonderful just by the beauty of her smile.

To David Heitz, Mike Stone, Joe Phelps, Tom Burgess, David and Nancy Garden, Keith and Marion Bowers, Mike and Tanya Grgich, Bill and Barbara Lincoln, Charles Wagner, Bernard Portet, Jerry Draper, Chuck Carpy, Jack Stuart, Mike and Mary Ellen Golick, Susan and Mike Robbins, and to the many people who took me by the hand and showed me the splendors of the Napa Valley, my sincere and heartfelt thanks.

The second edition of this book brought me back to my beloved Valley a decade later to refurbish old friendships and bask in the warmth of new ones. Bernard and Evelyn Skoda won an unassailable spot in my affections, as did John and Bett Shafer. A chance meeting with Tony Peju resulted in three delightful evenings, complete with a very outstanding Sauvignon Blanc. Peter and Su Wah Newton not only shared the spectacular beauty of their stunning new home with me, but were at all times the best, most considerate hosts or tennis partners. Newell and JoAnn DePuy were, as always, completely delightful company. To all those people, who eased the burden of loneliness and spared me from the horrors of my own cookery, I give my sincere thanks.

I have intentionally saved till last my expressions of appreciation to Joe and Alice Heitz and to my wife Gertie, for without their help this book would still be an unfulfilled dream. Joe and Alice not only gave me their unqualified help, but also their friendship. Their delightful little guest house ("Tobacco Road West," I believe a former occupant had named it) became for me the "Heitz Hilton" and sheltered me for a total of well over two months. It was not only shelter, but also a place where I knew there would be good food, companionship, and wine such as few people are ever privileged to drink; but mostly, it was a place where I knew I would be with good friends.

Right from the beginning, Joe and Alice have given this project their boundless help and enthusiasm. Here I have met people from all over the world and tasted superb wines poured with a lavish hand, for no one drinks better wine than Joe Heitz, unless it is his guests. It is only fitting and proper that this book should be dedicated to Joe and Alice, for no one has helped more in its making. But, then, these are my friends. To them, helping anyone is second nature, but helping a friend is a primary impulse.

The most difficult part of writing, I am told, is to express feelings that are so deep and basic that words somehow seem painfully inadequate; and so it is when I try to say "Thank You" to my wife, Gertie. Throughout the making of this book, she has been my rock of refuge. She has helped, encouraged, bolstered and solaced me with the suggestions and gentle understanding that only a good wife who is your other half can provide.

For the many hours spent at a typewriter trying to decipher my sometimes frenetic scrawl, for lawns laboriously mowed in my absence, for the many precious days and nights we could have had together but didn't because this book had to be done, for all the wonderful things you are...

I don't have to say it because you know, as always, what is in my heart.

Earl Roberge ASMP
Walla Walla, Washington

INTRODUCTION

When Noah looked around somewhere east of Ararat for the best possible site for his vineyard, he not only started an industry, but also initiated a search that has gone on to this day with unabated vigor. Over the centuries, special places favored with the right combination of soil, climate, moisture and elevation have become highly prized — to the point that many wars have been fought and much blood shed to secure these lands.

The Bordeaux region of France, the fabled hills of Burgundy, and the terraced slopes of the Rheingau are world famous simply because they have demonstrated over a span of many centuries that they can consistently yield a superior wine, not because of some isolated fortunate accident, but the predictable result of a happy set of circumstances duplicated in very few places in the world.

Over a long span of time, a store of facts and legends has collected around these areas. They have become renowned in song and verse as happy lands where the work is hard and exacting, but also as places where the earth gratefully receives the kiss of the sun, and when lovingly caressed, is generous with her favors.

The history of wine is so interwoven with the history of man it would be futile to try to separate them. No one knows with any certainty when the first wine was made; more likely than not it was the result of some happy accident. Some prehistoric caveman, on visiting his store of previously harvested grapes, probably found that some of them had become crushed, releasing a juice that miraculously had been changed into a liquid not only delicious to the taste, but which induced a euphoria previously unknown. Certainly it was known to the ancient Egyptians and Sumerians. The odes of Homer are replete with references to it, and the Phoenicians made it a principal item of commerce. There are 167 references to wine in the Bible — mostly complimentary, for in an area where water was either scarce or contaminated, wine was a safe, delightful beverage, considered very much part of everyday life. The Jewish Sabbath observance features wine; it is no coincidence that when Jesus Christ, at the Last Supper, commanded His disciples to repeat that sacred rite, He chose as its symbols bread and wine, the everyday staples that were the mainstays of life.

The flowering of the Roman Empire gave wine and viticulture a tremendous impetus, since the Romans soon found that one of the best ways to stabilize and civilize nomadic tribes was to engage them in raising grapes. The hard labor attendant to the practice of viticulture not only burned off energy otherwise dissipated in warfare, but it also bound the people to one spot. It takes years to successfully propagate a vineyard, and no one is about to leave an endeavor that has occupied a major portion of one's adult life. So, we see the Roman Emperors settling their veterans in the provinces, granting them riverfront sites in Cisalpine Gaul and along the Danube, where they would raise vineyards that were to become the most prolific in the Empire.

In A.D. 92, the Emperor Domitian, fearful of the competition of the provincial vineyards over those of Italy, ordered all vineyards in Cisalpine Gaul to be uprooted. The Emperor's edict was honored more in the breach than it was in fact, for by this time the local governors were beginning to realize the true worth of the

Above: Towering over the Northern Valley, Mt. St. Helena is the central theme. Once heavily wooded, it was almost totally denuded by a disastrous forest fire in 1964, but is now once more sprouting its usual coat of evergreens. *Right:* nestled amidst its leaves of green, crimson and gold, a cluster of Napa Gamay grapes await the hand of the picker. *Overleaf:* From the top of the mountain near Angwin, evening twilight dyes the fog banks over the Pacific and outlines in golden light the mountain ridges that border the Napa Valley.

experiment that had primarily been intended to civilize a warlike people. In places under the direct control and supervision of the Emperor, the edict was more or less honored, but in the far-flung reaches of the Gaul there were many places where the word from Rome was either ignored or never received. In A.D. 293 the Emperor Probus, a more pragmatic ruler, donned the imperial purple, and the edict was rescinded. The desire for good wine was stronger than official decree, a lesson obviously lost on those who foisted the Prohibition Amendment on the American people.

By this time, a pattern was beginning to emerge. Certain lands raised better grapes than others; some regions raised certain varieties of grapes to a unique degree of excellence, while others were better suited to cereal crops or fruits. Already the Bordeaux region and Burgundy were being proclaimed the equal or superior to the more established wine lands of Italy or Northern Africa. It took some time for their preeminence to be established, but the process was already under way.

The discoveries of the late Middle Ages and the intellectual ferment induced by the Renaissance also added to the interest in new wine lands. The island of Madeira was discovered and found to be very good wine country; and with the coming of the white man to America, a whole new chapter unfolded.

The first European settlers to the New World brought vine cuttings from their homelands. While the original interest was mainly in producing wine for the celebration of the Mass, it soon became apparent that some areas of the New World were well suited to the grape. Viticulture became one of the main efforts of the missionaries, especially of the indefatigable Franciscans. The vine followed the missions, and in California it found its most fertile ground. The versatile, if somewhat plebian, Mission grape was planted at most of the missions along El Camino Real, and formed the basis for the present wine industry in California.

The measure of any wine producing region is the quality of its product. Measured by this infallible standard, there is one region that should stand as an equal, or even as a superior, to the better-known wine lands of the world; but like the fabled younger sister in the Cinderella story, it is still to be fully noticed or appreciated. However, observers with discerning eyes are already predicting that this young land will someday eclipse her older sisters, once her beauty has fully matured and is made known to a waiting world. This is the Napa Valley in North Central California, a land created on a day when God was in a particularly good mood.

The Napa Valley becomes a wide plain where it bathes its feet in the salt water of San Pablo Bay. At Carneros at the southern end, the Valley is still mostly flat with a few hills giving a promise of what is to be. As it marches inland, the Valley narrows; the surrounding hills have become small mountains, progressively more densely wooded; and soon, at Yountville, it has narrowed to a width of only three miles.

The character of the land likewise has been changing, for although Highway 29, which skirts the western edge of the Valley, is bordered by vineyards almost as soon as it leaves the city limits of Napa, it now is practically surrounded by them. From Yountville to the north, the Valley is dedicated wholeheartedly to viticulture. Vineyards are everywhere, filling practically every acre in the

Above: An 1890 period winery, Far Niente, has been restored to its original splendor and is once more making good wine. *Right:* In the early morning on the Yount Mill Road, it is easy to understand why this region had such a hold on George Yount that, with the whole Valley at his feet, he chose this part for his home. *Overleaf:* Framed in a tangle of azaleas and a flowering plum tree, the Napa Valley slumbers under a blanket of fog with only the tops of the firs poking through the mist. This scene is from Tom and Linda Burgess's backyard.

erously lavished on this region—a beauty which has inspired artists, photographers, poets and writers, and made this Valley one of the most sought-after home sites in the world.

It is the story of this beautiful Valley that I would like to tell in this book. If I seem a bit fulsome in my praise, please remember that my association with it, as is the case with most visitors, has been more in the nature of a love affair than a marriage. One may condone, or even find endearing, faults in a mistress that would be intolerable in a wife; and the Valley is a lovely mistress—seductive, alluring, and promising in her lush beauty all manner of earthly delights. She is also, as those who live here will tell you, a wonderful wife—merry, hard working, bountiful, and forgiving; so those who have succumbed to her charms gladly spend a lifetime here, and with their dying breath question whether the glories of a promised Paradise hereafter can possibly eclipse those of the one in which they have spent their earthly lives.

Telling the full story of such a place is patently impossible; that would take several lifetimes, nor do I delude myself that I am qualified to do so. All I can do is show and tell of the things I have experienced and observed in my all-too-short stay in this Valley. I make no pretense of being an expert on any phase of life here; I am only an interested, sympathetic and observant viewer who experienced a small part of this way of life and found it to be very, very good indeed.

As for the wine scene, that is basic to this Valley. Although it is true that there are people living in the Valley who—mostly because of religious convictions—take no part in the manufacture or consumption of the Valley's most important product economically, it still remains an irrefutable fact that the main business of the Valley is the growing of wine grapes and the making of table wines. Trying to narrate the story of the Napa Valley without telling about these things would be like trying to describe Detroit without ever once mentioning the automobile industry.

Another fact should be made crystal clear: I make no pretense of being a wine expert, a fact which daily becomes more clear to me as I associate with people who are. While I have an excellent cellar, and under the tutelage of some very expert tasters have developed a rather discriminative palate, I do not feel myself qualified to pass judgment on the relative merits of the various wines I have tasted in this Valley. Suffice it to say, my interest in wine and in the places where it is produced has taken me to most of the places on this earth where good wines are made, not the least of which is the Napa Valley. Certainly, no place has consistently offered me better wine.

In case you're thinking of loading all your worldly possessions onto a truck and heading for the Napa Valley, it's only fair to tell you that those beautiful hills also grow a luxuriant crop of poison oak; the rattlesnakes are downright unsocial; the drinking water, to put it kindly, is somewhat less than ideal; traffic on Highway 29 is a weekend nightmare; real estate prices are astronomical and still rising; living costs are soaring; holding ponds sometimes exude a highly fetid odor; and one must drive sixty miles or so to reach the conveniences of a large metropolitan area.

Somehow, this doesn't seem to deter the flood of people seeking to settle here. Napa Valley was threatened

Above: Miljenko "Mike" Grgich is world famous for his Chardonnay. *Right:* The old Bale Mill was built in 1846 and for many years ground grist and flour. It is now a major tourist attraction with its forty-foot overshot wheel, which is one of the more popular targets for visiting camera buffs.

with a fate similar to the Santa Clara Valley where one of the most beautifully fertile agricultural areas in California was inexorably swallowed up by urbanization. So, in 1968, an agricultural preserve was established for Napa County, very strictly delineating the conditions under which homes and industries could be built in the Valley. The result has been that from the city of Napa northward the Valley is still mostly agricultural, and wineries seeking to expand almost drown in a sea of paperwork before they can increase their output. Vineyards seem to have less trouble getting permission, so occasionally the industry suffers from a surplus of grapes, especially of choice varietals from newly planted vineyards just now coming into production. This surplus of grapes presents a problem—in this case too much of a good thing. Wineries have to be expanded to house the additional stores of wine; and consumption must be increased, which is not always feasible in the face of rising prices, before this problem is solved. Of course, there will never be a real surplus of the best wines; the total production of the whole Valley is too limited to ever have that happen. Napa Valley wines are always in demand, but local and national conditions can create temporary problems, the solution of which can add a few wrinkles to the harried vintner's brow.

Every few miles along Highway 29, towns are strung like beads on a necklace. These towns are small—and stay small by choice. Yountville is growing eastward, but seems to be well stabilized. Oakville and Rutherford are the very small sites of sizable wineries, while St. Helena seems quite content to remain what it is—a rural, quiet town with vintage 1915 streetlights and well used parks, pages out of a more sedate chapter in American life. Most of these small towns glory in their smallness and have absolutely no intention of ever achieving the growth that has transformed so much of California into a characterless suburbia.

The one exception to this rule seems to be Calistoga. In 1974, the population was hovering around 2,000. In 1984 it was over double that and growing. Calistoga evidently has adopted the growth that St. Helena has eschewed, and, for good or evil, inevitably has been changed in the process.

Unlike the great wine producing areas of Europe, the Napa Valley has a comparatively short wine producing history. The Franciscan missionaries led the way when in 1823 Father José Altimira and an armed escort of Mexican soldiers visited the Valley, looking for a site that would complete the chain of missions started by Father Juniperro Serra. Father Altimira finally chose his mission site at Sonoma, where the church he established is today the well visited Mission San Francisco Solano. He did, however, record his visit to the Napa Valley in such glowing terms that it shortly became the mecca of settlers seeking new wildernesses to conquer.

There is no doubt that it was a wilderness. Part of it was a swamp, teeming with waterfowl and crisscrossed by myriad creeks and sloughs. Much of the Valley was covered with veritable groves of oak trees, and alive with game. Archaeological excavations have shown that this Valley has had a continuous occupancy by native Americans for over four thousand years, and it is safe to conjucture that nature's bounty had much to do with their presence. The Indians not only lived very well from this provident land, but also found in the hot springs and

Above: The basis of the great Johannisberg Riesling of Germany, the White Riesling grape yields, in the Napa Valley, a fruity semi-sweet wine. Next to Chardonnay, this is probably the most popular white wine produced in this country. *Right:* A volcanic upheaval probably caused this rocky knoll in the Valley. In spite of the difficulties attendant to building on sites like this, they are favored spots because of the beautiful views they afford.

mud baths that bubble so profusely from the base of Mt. St. Helena a cure for the multiple aches and pains that always seem to plague a primitive culture. They were generally a peaceful, unwarlike people — clean, moral and with a high regard for the beautiful realm that was their home. Unfortunately, these qualities are no match for the steel and greed of a technologically superior culture. So these original Valley inhabitants were an easy prey to the white men who soon flocked in to work the land grants Mexico was so eager to bestow on loyal citizens willing to develop this new land.

The white man brought not only a new way of life, he also brought his diseases against which the Indian had no natural immunity. Smallpox was the most virulent killer, although cholera and venereal diseases also decimated this once happy people. In the century since the coming of the white man, the original several thousand natives have dwindled down to a comparative handful. Stone artifacts and beautifully chipped arrowheads from the obsidian of Glass Mountain are about the only sign they ever lived here, although the present name of the Valley itself is of Indian origin.

The Napa Valley fell within the administrative jurisdiction of General Mariano Vallejo, the urbane Mexican military governor whose headquarters were at nearby Sonoma. He was under instructions from his superiors to maintain order, collect taxes, and develop the land. To this end, almost any loyal citizen of Mexico with the right connections, who indicated he could, and would, carve a productive, tax-paying ranch from the wilderness, found the acquisition of land not too difficult. The big problem was finding the labor necessary to work such an establishment. The Indians were docile enough, and when correctly supervised made reasonably good agricultural workers. They were, however, inclined to have a rather relaxed attitude toward hard physical labor — especially when the hunting and the fishing were so good. These pragmatists could see no valid reason to sweat in the fields when Nature's bounty was all around them, free for the taking. It took a special type of man to handle them, and that man soon put in an appearance, coming on the scene just at the time when the tides of agriculture, already well established in neighboring Sonoma Valley, were lapping closer and closer to the lush Napa Valley.

This region has produced more than its share of memorable characters, but, with the possible exception of the legendary Sam Brannan, none more colorful than George Calvert Yount.

A native of North Carolina, Yount was part of that restless horde that pushed westward in the early part of the nineteenth century, always looking for a new frontier. He was a man of his time — energetic, innovative, resourceful, fifty years a pioneer. When in 1831 he first viewed the whole Napa Valley (reportedly after climbing an Indian trail to the top of Mt. St. Helena), he saw a spectacle that must have moved him to the very depths of his soul. The Valley was wearing its spring vestments, a bright splash of color from the flowering mustard weed that painted it in a streak of yellow-gold. Instinctively, he knew that his search for a place where he could put down roots was over, that in this beautiful Valley he would live and die. He got his wish. Under an imposing granite shaft, the remains of George Yount today rest in Yountville, a Valley town named in his honor.

Above: The work is hot, and that lug of grapes weighs forty pounds, but there's always time for a smile. *Right:* The day ends over the western mountains, bathing the Valley in a golden haze. Twilight and dawn are magical times in the Valley.

In General Vallejo, the cultured governor of this region, he found a kindred spirit; and this oddly assorted pair soon became fast friends. Yount had little in the way of material possessions, but he had the resourcefulness of the pioneer and the uncanny trading ability of the frontiersman. One story of how he built his fortune relates that he once showed the general how the redwood trees growing in the sheltered mountain valleys of his domains could be readily transformed into shingles that were lighter and generally superior to the baked tile then used in roofing. The general's gratitude took the form of a grant stretching for miles, the Rancho Caymus, which now constitutes a good part of the Napa Valley. Yount lived the usual good life of the Spanish land grant rancher, raising cattle, sheep — and grapes, which the general converted to wine in his Mission style winery.

The practice of viticulture was not new in California. The very earliest Franciscan missionaries brought with them cuttings of the Mission grape, which had thrived so mightily in Mexico that the reigning Spanish overlords once had them uprooted because their production threatened the livelihood of Spanish vintners. The highly productive Mission grape, which never yielded a great beverage, was imported to make wine for the Mass. Since crushing was achieved by having Indians dance barefooted on a mass of grapes piled onto a stretched cowhide, and fermentation took place in skin bags with the hair turned inward, there may have been a few reasons other than the quality of the grapes why the wine never achieved a high degree of popularity. But it was wine, and in lieu of something better it had to do.

As in the days of ancient Rome, the vineyard workers were the natives. Their work produced not only wine, after a fashion, but also a side benefit: it helped stabilize a sometimes nomadic population; drew off their excess energy in agriculture, rather than warfare; and by binding them to the soil, helped accelerate the process of "civilization." Shades of the Roman emperors! The very same reasons had been applied, eighteen centuries before, to settle and civilize the then warlike tribes of Gaul — and in the process produced the people who were to become the world's finest vintners.

Probably because he was himself a frontiersman and had a thorough knowledge of Indian culture, Yount got along very well with them and in a short time was able to make them skilled vineyard workers. His vineyards flourished, especially since it soon became very apparent that, due to some happy natural circumstance, his grant of land constituted an area supremely well adapted to the raising of superior grapes. The qualities that were to make the Napa Valley world famous had been discovered.

The next twenty years or so were pretty hectic, for the rush of Forty-niners to the gold fields of the Mother Lode Country spilled over into the Valley and almost overnight changed the character of the region. These people had a tendency to blandly ignore property lines; and since they were apt to be a bit careless as well as extremely adept with firearms, the process of removing them from the land was sometimes highly interesting. Then, too, the transition from Mexican to American sovereignty resulted in legal difficulties, disputed land grants, and general uncivility. But somehow by 1860, the problems had been resolved, and the Valley was ready to assume its rightful role.

Above: A basket of grapes and a freshly opened bottle of Chardonnay are natural adjuncts to a party in the Napa Valley, as are these at Bob Wood's party to celebrate the first crush of the season. *Right:* A young man practices a very ancient art at the Robert Mondavi Winery; a young cooper assembles barrel staves of Navarre oak imported from France. The tools he is using have changed little in 4,000 years. *Overleaf:* From the top of Pritchard Hill the eye roams over acres of beautifully tilled vineyards to Mt. St. Helena, towering in the distance.

The 1860s saw an influx of European wine makers, usually cultured, knowledgeable men who indelibly stamped the future character of the Valley. The word of this new wine producing region must have reached Germany first, because the initial wave of vintners were mostly Germans. Charles Krug came in 1858, and in 1861 established a solidly built stone winery, part of which still stands to this day. In 1862, Jacob Schram cleared mountain land and planted the vines that were to firmly establish Schramsberg as one of the outstanding wineries of California. The Beringer brothers, Jacob and Frederic, were comparative latecomers; but they brought with them the kind of wine making they had learned in the Medoc, and profoundly affected the style of viticulture in the Valley. Frederic also brought a style of living whose effect can be felt to this day. On the outskirts of St. Helena, fronting the extensive caves of his winery, he erected a replica of the ancestral home in Mainz, Germany. Resplendent with carved oak and cut glass, it has been beautifully restored to the glory that once made it the social center of St. Helena.

By 1880, wine making was firmly established as the major occupation of the Valley. No less than six hundred vineyards flourished, and from Napa to Calistoga the Valley was clothed in a mantle of vigorously growing vines. In spite of the economic upheavals of the 1870s, the future seemed golden indeed. Napa Valley wines were already establishing their reputation for excellence; the market, though erratic, was good and getting better; and although the industry always had its share of problems, no one could foresee anything but an increasingly prosperous future. Then, disaster struck.

Imagine the consternation of a vineyardist who has worked ten years or more to establish his vigorously healthy vines, only to see them suddenly dry up and die. On pulling up a dying vine, he finds that the root system has been systematically riddled. It has been destroyed, underground, by a pest so small that it can barely be seen by the naked eye, but the staggering damage that *phylloxera vastatrix* caused was all too apparent! The vine louse probably reached California on the cuttings imported from Europe by Count Agoston Haraszthy, but paradoxically was of American origin. The only known method of combating this underground menace was flooding the vineyards long enough to drown the pest, but not long enough to rot the vines. While this method may sometimes have been feasible in Europe, it was essentially impractical in Napa Valley, a region noted neither for an excess of water nor flat land. So, many a fine vineyard was uprooted and planted to grass.

The cure was discovered just in time to keep the infant industry from foundering. It was learned that while phylloxera loves the roots of the vinifera grapes, it could not damage the roots of the native American vines. Adaptation through the centuries probably is the reason for this most fortuitous circumstance. The noble grapes of the Old World could be, and were, successfully grafted to the native American rootstock; and within ten years the vineyards were flourishing again. The vineyardists breathed a sigh of relief. Certainly, they thought, nothing could be worse than phylloxera and the financial panics that plagued the era.

They were wrong.

On October 18, 1919, to the utter disbelief of this wine producing area, the 18th Amendment, which pro-

Above: Charles Carpy's grandfather helped to establish the wine industry in the Napa Valley. Now he carries on the family tradition as one of the partners in Freemark Abbey. *Right:* The end of the day is close. Placido has done a full day's work with skill and endurance. *Overleaf:* A short distance off the Silverado Trail on a side road leading to Stags' Leap Winery, the vineyards run abruptly into the eastern mountain wall.

hibited the manufacture, sale, or transportation of intoxicating liquor, was ratified and became national law — even in the Napa Valley. To a people for whom wine was a staple and a way of life, this was complete madness — a well intentioned, but senseless, completely unworkable regulation whose only function seemed to be the ruination of the work of generations and to make anyone a lawbreaker who did any part of that work.

Any law, to be functional, must have the support of the general populace, and in no section of the United States was the Prohibition Amendment more enthusiastically ignored than in the Napa Valley. It seemed no Italian ever could be convinced that this was really the law of the land and that in ignoring it he was committing a serious crime. However, after a few painful incidents, it finally dawned on the growers that this was not some monstrous practical joke; they were indeed breaking the law by practicing the art that had been handed down to them by their ancestors for two thousand years. Sadly, they began to convert their beautifully tended vineyards to prune and walnut orchards.

To be sure, some wineries, especially those that had wisely specialized in sacramental and medicinal wines kept going all through Prohibition, keeping alive the art of the vintner. Then, too, the hills around St. Helena and Calistoga are rugged and not too easily accessible to those not familiar with them. Old timers will tell you stories of tank car loads of molasses moving into the Valley — every two or three days — to be fermented and distilled into 190 proof alcohol that could be cut back to potable strength. Stills were everywhere, and the heady odor of fermenting wine that had formerly clothed the Valley was replaced by the equally heady odor of fermenting mash and distilled moonshine. Very heavy coffins, followed by sad faced mourners, routinely went to Santa Rosa to be placed on the train to San Francisco. Of course, those coffins sloshed a bit when jostled and the same mourners attended each funeral, a fact that was dutifully pointed out by a local man who was doing his last two years in federal service before claiming his pension. Following his cue, the mourners were changed — and he lived to claim his pension.

Those barely accessible mountain vineyards really came into their own during Prohibition. Many a fine vintage was gathered, crushed and fermented in the dark of the moon, so when the national madness passed in 1933, there some well aged wines on hand to toast its unlamented demise.

There is no denying that Prohibition did more damage to the Napa Valley than even the phylloxera beetle. Beautifully tended vineyards of prime varietal grapes were ripped up to be replanted with prunes or walnuts — or sowed to pasture grass. Vacated wineries fell into disrepair or were converted to other uses. Irreplaceable old cooperage fell apart and was lost forever. A vineyard that produces no grapes, or a winery that makes no wine, is an exercise in futility. These were undeniable disasters, but the bigger loss was in people. An unemployed vintner must necessarily find other work if he is to survive, and skills unused for fourteen years can become so atrophied their revival is questionable. Also, good vineyard workers are not produced overnight. A whole generation of skilled workers in fine varietal grapes was lost, and those who survived by tending the Alicante Bouschet grape lost a virtue very important to a skilled

Above: Bill Cadman doesn't have one of the larger wineries in the Valley, but he does have one of the better ones. *Right:* An old remodeled winery has been turned into a charming warren of shops, boutiques and restaurants at Yountville's charmingly reconstructed Vintage 1870 complex.

craftsman — his pride in his work. This tough-skinned but quite plebeian grape largely supplanted the more delicate varietal grapes because it could stand the rigors of transportation even to the East Coast. There it was used for home wine making, which was legal under this peculiar law. The Alicante was also a great favorite with bootleggers because its blood-red juice imparted a lot of color to the wine; therefore, it could be liberally "cut" with adulterants and still present a passable color to the undiscerning eye. Large quantities of this very inferior wine were consumed, tending to set standards so low that when the horrible post-Prohibition wines arrived, they were accepted, if not with enthusiasm, at least with varying degrees of resignation.

Another, if somewhat intangible loss, was the general disregard for law engendered by Prohibition. People who had never before broken a major law now did so with little or no compunction, a habit which inevitably spread to all fields of endeavor, business and social. Gangsters accumulated huge fortunes and invested them in extralegal enterprises, operating behind the shield of bought public officials and judges. The general decline in morality that began during Prohibition seeded a bitter harvest, the effects of which are still with us today and influence our everyday lives. Those fourteen years of Prohibition can truly be called the Napa Valley's—and America's—Dark Age.

The aftermath of Prohibition was almost as ruinous to the industry as the law itself had been. The great thirst engendered by the long dry spell had to be quenched somehow, so wines whose only distinction was that they had a very high alcohol content were rushed into production. People who had never tasted wine before may very well be excused if, when tasting some of those first efforts, they concluded they had not been missing very much. Cheaply made, poorly aged wines undeniably sold, but also created a negative reaction that set back for many years the general acceptance of wine as a worthwhile experience.

However, along with the poor wines, some good and even great wines were being laid down. Now that wine production could function legally, new wineries were opened, modern methods were introduced, and the foundations for the Valley's present high standards were formulated. Wineries proliferated, and every year more and more acreage in the Valley was dedicated to grape growing. The process of 1919 was now reversed; extensive, well established groves of prunes and walnuts were torn out and the ground painstakingly prepared for vines that would supply the grapes wineries needed to supply an ever expanding market. The modern era of the Napa Valley had begun.

A few far sighted vintners as far back as 1943 had already perceived the obvious. The future of the Valley should rest on the solid base of quality rather than quantity. After all, even if all the arable land in the Valley were planted to grapes, there would be a total of only about 25,000 acres—an area that could comfortably be tucked into a forgotten corner of Bordeaux. By this time, all sections of the Valley had been planted to grapes of one variety or another, and a pattern began to emerge. The three hundred or so microclimates into which the Valley is divided were beginning to be discovered and to assert themselves. Some sections raised exceptional Zinfandel; others, through some unique chemistry, did

Above: One of the most overlooked floral displays in botanical history is the flowering of the grape, here shown larger than life size. However, without this insignificant looking display, there would be no ripe grapes in September. *Right:* Under an arch of olive trees planted a hundred years ago by Jacob Schram, the Jack Davies family, present owners of Schramsberg, head happily back home after a day's outing in the vineyards.

Left: Doing what comes naturally at his age, a youngster gets a boy's-eye view of the Napa Valley. *Above:* After all the juice has been extracted from the must, there is still use for the residue. Called "pomace," it makes an excellent, as well as colorful, vineyard fertilizer. *Overleaf:* While it looks like something transplanted from an Aegean isle, Sterling Vineyards Winery is really an ultramodern complex, dedicated to the making of good wine. It was also designed to give the tourist a good idea of how wine is made.

CHAPTER I

LAND OF THE SMOKING EARTH, CALISTOGA

When you consider that Calistoga was founded by the empire-building Sam Brannan, you have a right to expect something out of the ordinary. Sam was the stuff of which legends are spun, and the town he founded naturally is as distinctive and unique as he was. A beautifully situated small town of 5,000 delightfully chauvinistic souls, it sits at the head of the Napa Valley with Mt. St. Helena towering in its backyard. Deservedly proud of its legendary past, it is perfectly content with its very agreeable present and serenely confident of its promising future.

Sam Brannan certainly thought it had a good future; with the whole West to choose from, he chose this spot to crown the career that had made him, at 28, California's first millionaire and as intriguing a figure as this picturesque Valley has ever produced. A renegade Mormon, he found horse racing, wine drinking, and wooing the prettiest women in the West more to his liking than hard manual work. He was also a charismatic leader, a far sighted entrepreneur, the possessor of a raffish if somewhat ebullient charm, and a very hard worker whenever the labor happened to be to his liking. Sam was first and foremost a promoter, one of that breed of men who carved an empire out of a wilderness and indelibly stamped a region with the brand of his personality. In the Calistoga region, he saw a chance to crown his career with an enterprise in keeping with the flamboyance that had carried him to fame and fortune.

The Indians had for centuries used the mud baths and geothermal springs that bubble from the base of Mt. St. Helena as a remedy for arthritic pain. It was therefore a popular gathering spot — in theory a place where tribal animosities were suspended, or at least curtailed, but in actual fact the scene of many a pitched battle. Because of the many thermal springs, some of them gushing plumes of live steam, the Indians referred to this area as "The Land Of The Smoking Earth."

The potential for recreation and development was tremendous, but it took a man of Brannan's vision and enthusiasm to transform the potential into his version of reality. The fact that he had six million dollars to pour into the venture certainly didn't hurt any. A good part of that money was definitely needed, for when Sam dreamed, he dreamed on a big scale — and what he envisioned was a spa to rival any then in existence. Starting in 1860, he poured money into a complex of swimming pools, cottages, mud baths and roller skating rinks. Avenues planted with palm trees led to the various parts of the estate and to the race track where his blooded Arabian horses regularly ran in the wildest races the Valley has ever seen. The whole place was designed to attract the newly rich aristocracy of San Francisco, and no money was spared to build a place where they would feel at home.

The aristocracy of San Francisco stayed away in droves. Sam's reputation as a lady's man, carouser, and general hell-raiser was not exactly the mark of distinction that the newly respectable elite of the Bay City craved. True, many of them spent a surreptitious week or two at Brannan's and went home wonderfully refreshed, but the place never did receive the cachet of respectabil-

Above: Hanns Kornell could easily delegate this task to someone else, but he personally examines each bottle of champagne by the traditional method — viewing the refracted light of candle flame through the wine to be sure it meets his exacting standards for clarity and lack of deposit. *Right:* At Hanns Kornell's Larkmead Lane champagne cellars, over four million bottles of fine sparkling wine rest and bottle age. Periodically, Hanns inspects, tests and tastes, to make sure than his "children" are growing up properly.

ity Sam so earnestly sought . . . at least, not during his lifetime. After he left the operation, it became quite the gathering place for people not only from the Bay area, but from the whole country.

There are several stories of how the town got its name. Before Brannan's time, the settlement had been named "Agua Caliente," an obvious reference to the many hot water springs in the area. The most common story tells how the round of celebrations marking the opening of the new resort obviously entailed the consumption of other, stronger waters; during the course of a decidedly bibulous dedication, Brannan proposed a toast to the new enterprise, "The Saratoga of California." His usually nimble tongue somewhat paralyzed by the local wine, it came out as "Calistoga of Sarafornia." The intriguing name stuck.

For forty years Calistoga was a popular resort, if not with the elite of California, at least with enough people to spread its fame liberally. People took the train from a landing on San Pablo Bay and traveled the length of the lovely Napa Valley to Calistoga. On returning, they brought back with them one of the habits contracted at Brannan's resort, a taste for the local wine. Sam Brannan had early realized the Valley's potential for producing fine wine, and by the mid 1860s his vineyards were the Valley's finest, boasting of 125,000 vines. With his usual business acumen, he certainly saw to it that his wines were served in the right places; and while the San Francisco aristocracy may have looked askance at Sam and his escapades, they readily accepted the quality of what he bottled. Napa Valley wines had an early acceptance in San Francisco in spite of the snobbery of the times that insisted nothing was as good as the best Bordeaux or Burgundy.

Although Calistoga has long ago ceded the title of "Wine Center of the Valley" to nearby St. Helena, it still maintains a lively interest in things vinous. On Tubbs Lake at the northern edge of the town, Chateau Montelena, an imposing French style chateau built by European stonemasons with imported stone, produces outstanding varietal wines. Beautifully situated on the edge of an artificial lake that boasts authentic Chinese pagodas, it is a delightful spot for a picnic, one that has yet to be fully discovered. A delightful place to visit any time of the year, but especially on a warm summer day, it is a cool oasis in an otherwise decidedly hot area.

At the southern end of Calistoga and some few miles down the Valley, Sterling Vineyards crowns a wooded knoll, looking like a picture out of an Aegean Sea travelogue. Certainly the most spectacular setting in the Valley, it was engineered to be not only a highly functional winery, but also a showplace where visitors could see all phases of wine making and storage on an unescorted tour. A monocable tramway feeds visitors to the attractively situated tasting room and also serves the function of keeping the too casual visitor at the bottom of the mountain. The view from the terraces of Sterling is the best in the whole Valley and worth in itself the cost of the trip. Sterling produces excellent varietal wines that are available at the winery and in selected California restaurants, although some wines will be marketed through distributors as this winery achieves its full potential.

On the eastern edge of the Valley near the Silverado trail, the comparatively new Cuvaison Winery, an out-

Above: At the Charles Krug Winery a gondola load of red grapes is tipped into the crusher by a movable hoist. The screw at the bottom of the crusher will feed the grapes into the crushing mechanism where the fruit is pulped. *Right:* The barrel-aging room at Sterling Vineyards is a study in symmetry. In this small cooperage, wines sleep, sometimes for years, until they gain the smoothness and character that oak supplies so graciously.

standing piece of functional Mission-style architecture, nestles into the hillside, looking as through it had grown there, so beautifully have its lines been integrated with the surrounding terrain.

Most of the Calistoga area wineries take advantage of the fact that red wine grapes attain a high sugar content at this end of the Valley, probably because climatically the north end of the Valley is much warmer. The south end is cooled, morning and evening, by the fogs off San Pablo Bay, so does not ripen grapes as quickly as does the more sunshiny north end. Also, the rocks rimming Calistoga retain the afternoon heat, and by radiating it long into the evening, hasten the ripening process by providing a high and long caloric intake. Some grapes, Zinfandel for instance, seem to do better on slopes — and there are slopes all around Calistoga.

Some of those slopes become rather precipitous. Mt. St. Helena itself is a semi-extinct volcano with some very abrupt escarpments; the mountains ringing the Valley to the east are sheer rock cliffs many hundreds of feet high. This accounts for the fact that Calistoga is a sailplaning center. On any warm day these graceful long-winged gliders can be seen effortlessly wheeling and soaring in a breathtakingly beautiful ballet as they seek the rising thermals that will give them altitude.

Not all the wines produced in this area are red. The road leading from Calistoga to St. Helena offers such an intriguing and ever-changing panorama that you could be forgiven if you miss the side road to the right with a simple sign beside it that says in elegant cursive script "Schramsberg." That would be your loss, for although the Valley is an undeniably beautiful jewel, there are also facets in the foothills that are equally brilliant. Schramsberg is one of these.

The original vineyard was hacked out of a mixed redwood, oak, and madrona forest by Jacob Schram, who in 1862 started a winery that soon established its reputation as one of the finest in California. When a casual visitor named Robert Louis Stevenson visited the place in 1880, he found a picture of prosperity, with a large Victorian mansion and extensive aging cellars carved hundreds of feet into the hillside. Phylloxera and Prohibition dealt the lovely old estate severe blows, but in 1964 Jack and Jamie Davies bought it and energetically set about restoring it. The place was a ruin, with bats in the attic and rats entrenched in the cellar, but today the old Victorian Mansion has been restored to a thing of beauty. The tunnels have been refurbished and enlarged, the mountain vineyards replanted — and Jack makes champagne that is pure gold. Using the original French *méthode champenoise*, he produces champagne from Pinot Noir, Pinot Chardonnay, Gamay and Flora grapes that has attracted worldwide interest, especially since personnel of the U.S. State Department have been known to order it for the very highest occasions. Jack's training in business management equips him well, for the distribution of his scarce champagne is as important as its production. Jacob Schram would be proud to see the estate today; it is in very capable hands.

On lyrically named Larkmead Lane, Hanns Kornell works his magic on four million or so bottles of fine champagne and proudly directs a very solvent empire founded on his skill as a wine maker and his value as a person. A refugee from Hitler's Germany, he is one of the outstanding successes of the Valley; for from his start

Above: Louis Martini carries on the tradition established by his late father, one of the greats in the industry. Here in his laboratory, he checks a wine with a very competent swirl of his glass. *Right:* From the heights of Sterling Vineyards, the Valley spreads its checkerboard of green, gold and crimson.

in 1940 to the present day, he has built the name "Kornell" into a synonym for fine champagne and staunch integrity. Those values have paid off. The newly enlarged storehouse and offices reflect the fact that some of America's finest champagnes are produced here and that the American public, increasingly sophisticated in matters vinous, readily accepts his product. His old stone winery, acquired in 1958, serves as a storehouse and aging cellar for fine wines, mostly Rieslings and Chardonnays which he buys from selected vintners. Using the methode champenoise, he transforms them into sparkling wines that have won many medals, even in competition with the most entrenched and respected champagnes of Europe.

There has been a substantial growth in new wineries in the decade between 1974 and 1984, but these represent such a major change in the character of the Valley — especially of the Calistoga area — that they will be treated at length in a later chapter.

Each part of the Napa Valley is different, has its own attraction, and is an integral part of that enchantment the Napa Valley as a whole weaves so effortlessly. Calistoga, with its Western style buildings, its plumes of geothermal steam, its air of living easily with a very lively past while courting an equally interesting future, is an intriguing place. What other town of 5,000 people can boast two Russian Orthodox churches, as well as having been founded by a renegade Mormon who was a con artist beyond compare? A walk through the hillside pioneer cemetery at the edge of town is a walk back into the nineteenth century; yet, lifting your eyes, you see, gliding gracefully in azure skies, sailplaines manned by bronzed young men and women who proudly call this place home and feel they have the best of all worlds.

It is seemingly paradoxical that Calistoga, at the very edge of the wine country and with a history of viticulture, should also be home to an excellent institution dedicated to the rehabilitation of those who have become too fond of the grape. It is part of the character of this town that seems to take the best from all facets of our culture, blended with its own particular style of living. In so doing, it produces a way of life that is an intrinsic and fascinating part of the Napa Valley.

Above: Through the open porch of Sterling Vineyards Winery, one sees the arches and architecture that have so often drawn comparisons between this winery and a Greek monastery. *Right:* Large oaken casks at Sterling Vineyards Winery store a wealth of aging wine, and bask dramatically in light streaming through the stained glass windows of the cellar.

Left: The hillside vineyards of Stony Hill are famous throughout the industry because they produce superlative Chardonnay. Production at this tiny winery is so limited, grapes are gathered in lug boxes and transported to the winery on the hood of a 1943 vintage Army Jeep, which is an ideal vehicle for this rugged terrain. *Above:* Jets of geothermal steam issue from pipes sunk into the ground at Pacheteau's Resort in Calistoga. The town was founded in 1860 by Sam Brannan, and remained a leading spa for many years. *Overleaf:* In the cool caves of Schramsberg, bins of upended bottles patiently sleep, letting their contents achieve the nobility which is their rightful due.

CHAPTER II

HEART OF THE VALLEY—ST. HELENA

It quite commonly happens that people seeing St. Helena for the first time fall helpless victims to its charm. For most, it is an unrequited love, and they return to their own homes with the memory of a pretty, leisurely paced little town that seems to have somehow escaped the frenetic rush of modern times and survived as an oasis of peace, quiet, and gracious living. Some determined souls do something about it, for many of the civic leaders of the town are people who have moved into it and found that while St. Helena indeed lives up to its first impression, it is a quality which is maintained only at the cost of considerable effort.

St. Helena didn't just happen; it is this way only because of the stamp put on it generations ago by the talented, hardworking men and women who made this their home and the scene of their labors. They established the delightful way of life that persists to this day; it remains as it is only because its present inhabitants appreciate that way of life and do as little as possible to disturb it.

A fortuitous accident of nature shaped St. Helena's destiny. The soil of the Napa Valley, composed as it is of volcanic dust, sedimentary deposits, and alluvial fans deposited in the Valley by the raging mountain streams, forms a terrain ideal for the growing of premium quality wine grapes. Add to this the happy chance that the amount of rainfall is usually just right and comes at the proper time, the balance of sunshine and fog is ideal, and numerous microclimates allow several varieties of fine wine grapes to thrive — and the town's future became predictable. It was foreordained that St. Helena should become the wine capital of California.

It undeniably is. This small town is home base for many a nationally known wine firm whose name is familiar to anyone who has ever shopped for a bottle of fine American wine.

It wasn't always thus. Back in the 1830s when the first white settlers began to enter the Valley, their main interest was more in cattle, not primarily for the meat, but for the hides and tallow. The many oak trees in the Valley provided the oak bark necessary for the tanning process, and "Napa Leather," most likely first made from deerskins, became a name in the trade that persists to this day. In 1846 Dr. Edward Turner Bale built his grist mill, still standing on the northern edge of St. Helena, which later ground poultry and livestock feed as well as flour for the bread hungry Forty-niners. The old mill with its giant overshot wheel is today a very popular tourist attraction, but in the days of its active life it was a symbol of the things that made life profitable, or even possible, in the Napa Valley.

A short distance south of the old Bale Mill, on the opposite side of the road, sits a handsome building of reddish cut stone. This is Freemark Abbey, which houses not only a nationally famous winery, but also a fine restaurant, a gift shop, and a candle factory whose artistic products are world famous. The building dates back to 1895 and an Italian named Antonio Forni, who, like most of the new arrivals from Italy, had wine on his mind. He built well. The old winery, which passed through many hands before being acquired in 1967 by the present

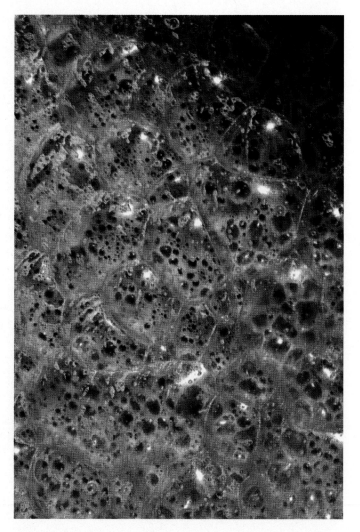

Above: New wine, still frothing from the carbon dioxide attendant to its birth, makes a swirling pink pattern in a wine sump. *Right:* An experimental pressing of Cabernet Franc at Spring Mountain Winery is part of the experimentation that is always going on at any good winery. Small batches, such as this, are pressed in basket presses rather than in the bladder presses customarily used for commercial loads. *Overleaf:* Jade Lake is a charming little oasis on Tubbs Lane, Calistoga, right next to Chateau Montelena. The islands boast authentic Chinese pagodas and chilled white wine is available only a few yards away. Welcome!

owners, has been equipped with the latest stainless steel fermentors and is busily fulfilling the reason for which it was originally built — making good wine.

In 1861 Charles Krug built his first permanent winery, north of St. Helena, where part of it stands to this day. The old buildings of greyish stone and stucco, blend perfectly with the background of oaks and spacious lawns. The old carriage house that formerly housed the winery's horses now holds hundreds of barrels of aging wine, and the main winery building holds huge tanks, some of redwood and others of glass-lined steel, most of them bigger than a railroad tank car.

The winery was acquired in 1943 by the late Cesare Mondavi. His son Peter supervises the company, one of the larger wineries in the Valley, and keeps an eagle eye on the quality that has made Charles Krug a name that means unvarying excellence.

Across the road from Charles Krug on a hillside overlooking the Valley, William Bourn, one of the richest men in America, in 1889 poured millions into a huge cut-stone building that is still the world's largest stone winery. An impressive, gray stone structure, it was somewhat damaged in the 1906 quake; legend has it that thousands of bottles of by now well-aged wines were buried when some of the tunnels collapsed. Acquired by The Christian Brothers in 1950, it served for many years as an aging cellar for their wines, as well as a bottling plant for their champagne. Age, smaller earthquakes, and the constant beat of myriad tourist feet took their toll, until the building was adjudged unsafe by The Brothers and closed to the public until extensive reinforcement work could be completed. It is an expensive as well as extensive renovation, dedicated to making the historic old building once more a productive unit in The Christian Brothers' chain of wineries, as well as a nostalgic link to the past.

Only a few hundred yards down the road is the famed Rhine House of the Beringer Brothers Winery. A copy of the ancestral home in Mainz, Germany, built of imported German oak and stained glass, it is one of the more impressive sights in the Napa Valley. The famed sandstone caves of the Beringers, patiently hacked out with pick and shovel by Chinese laborers, have been expertly restored and serve as aging cellars for the winery. They are unquestionably one of the more worthwhile tourist attractions of the Valley.

Since its acquisition by Nestle, Beringer has undergone much expansion and renovation. Besides restoring the famed caves, banks of new stainless steel fermentors flank each side of the road. The capacity of the winery has been greatly increased over the old days, but always with the aim of getting the very best quality out of the grapes grown in Beringer's extensive vineyards.

Across the Valley, just off the road to Angwin, Burgess Cellars, a delightfully situated old cut-stone winery, perches on a hillside overlooking its own vineyards, and enjoys a gorgeous view of the Valley, right from its own windows. On the opposite side of the Valley, Chateau Chevalier, a delightful replica of a French chateau, sits in a fold in a valley off the Spring Mountain Road. The owners worked long, hard hours to replant the mountain vineyards and restore the old estate. The grapes are crushed, fermented and aged in the cellar of the picturesque old chateau, which not only looks like a French wine cellar, but also functions as one.

Above: This avenue of elms, fronting the Rhine House in St. Helena, is a cool tunnel of verdure even on the hottest day. *Right:* The buildings of Rutherford Hill Winery, on the eastern slopes of the Valley, bask in the warm sun of late afternoon.

The largest home in St. Helena is the huge Victorian mansion erected on Spring Mountain in 1885 by Tiburcio Parrot, the son of the American consul in Mazatlan and a Mexican mother. A larger replica of the Rhine House, it sits on spacious landscaped grounds overlooking a swimming pool, providing a beautiful view of the Valley. Purchased in 1974 by Mike Robbins, a San Francisco businessman turned wine maker, it has been extensively renovated to house his Spring Mountain Winery, which formerly occupied the cellar of another large Victorian house he owned on the St. Helena Highway. On the Spring Mountain property is a large tunnel, dug ninety feet into the hillside, which affords a perfect spot for aging the Cabernets and Chardonnays that are already establishing an outstanding reputation for this fine winery.

While to the locals it is still known as the Parrot Estate, a much larger national audience knows it as Falcon Crest. In the popular TV series, it is the residence of the viperish Angela Channing who seems to spend more time at her multiple mechinations than she does making wine. This does not sit too well with many Valley residents who know that while the Valley probably has its share of shady characters, it also is the home of thousands of decent, hard working persons who resent being tarred with a hedonistic brush. Consequently, Falcon Crest does not rate as highly in the Valley as it does elsewhere; if you were to believe most of the people here, it is not very well watched. Since every episode is pretty well damned as soon as it is produced, it is also safe to surmise more sets are tuned to it than are generally acknowledged.

The ride up Spring Mountain Road is one of the prettiest originating in the Valley. Densely wooded most of the way, the road is a tunnel of cool verdure, with a lively creek noisily gamboling alongside. Each side road leads to a vineyard or winery, for this whole area is excellent grape growing country; owners of this choice land are not about to pass up the opportunities that come with the ownership of these coveted spots. The road finally tops the mountain and wanders off downhill to Santa Rosa.

St. Helena is home to two large cooperatives that crush an impressive part of the Valley's total crop. Their large, down-to-earth exteriors hide really impressive interiors well suited for their purpose, which is to make wine. The relics of an era more dedicated to efficiency than aesthetics, they are nevertheless an integral part of the wine complex in the Napa Valley.

On the southern edge of town is a low, very modern complex of buildings that house the warehousing and crushing facilities of The Christian Brothers. This crushing and fermenting complex is quite different in that it is circular, rather than following the more traditional rectangular concept. This innovative step has proven extremely practical and is always considered as a model whenever new crushing facilities are planned anywhere. Geared to mass production while still keeping all the good aspects of a smaller winery, this modern plant can crush thousands of tons of grapes in the same time most wineries would use to crush a hundred tons. Although it is the largest single facility in the Napa Valley, it is nevertheless only part of a planned complex that will some day move the greater part of The Brothers' facilities to South St. Helena.

Above: In his Spring Mountain Vineyard, Jerry Draper squeezes grape juice onto the plate of his refractometer to measure sugar content. *Right:* Charles Wagner, Jr., is a third generation Valley resident who has followed in his father's footsteps and carried on the family's wine-making tradition at Caymus Vineyards. Using a wine-thief, he samples a Cabernet that he had a hand in making.

Their neighbor down the road is the Louis Martini Winery, which is almost always a suprise to the visitor. The name is well known to most wine buffs, who know that for years the name Martini has stood for an always sound — and often great — wine at a reasonable price. The buildings were erected in 1933 in anticipation of the end of Prohibition and are simply no-nonsense, practical-type structures whose only function is to protect the wine making equipment from the elements. The elder Martini, who established this winery, was a legend in his own time — a hard working, knowledge-able, hospitable Italian who had a positive genius for producing fine wines. His son, Louis P. Martini, who has taken over the mantle of leadership, has apparently inherited his father's flair and embellished it with a few additional flourishes of his own. A large-framed, ener-getic man with a ready smile and a notable sense of humor, he is dedicated to carrying on a fine tradition and adding laurels to a name already extremely well respected in wine circles.

As is not uncommon in family-owned wineries, a new generation of wine makers and administrators is coming to the fore. In 1977, son Michael Martini, a graduate enologist of the University of California at Davis, took over as wine maker; daughter Carolyn is administrator; and youngest daughter Pat is chief financial officer. Louis looks in on the youngsters once in a while to make sure everything is running smoothly, but is gradually letting the younger generation take over while he savors his well-earned retirement.

Martini Winery has the usual complement of redwood tanks, only more so. It also has huge concrete vats, used for fermenting red wines, and many thousands of oak barrels, where red wines — and some whites — patiently sleep and take on the character and silkiness that oak seems to impart so beautifully. Throughout the industry the name is respected for the integrity and value it implies, for Martini's influence has done much to sta-bilize prices in this country. A firm believer in giving the customer his money's worth, he is making and selling good wine at a reasonable price ... and making a profit on it. The influence this has had on stabilizing prices is considerable, for Martini is one of the larger wineries in the Valley, with an output of more than 250,000 cases a year.

Across the street from Martini, Bob Trinchero oper-ates what used to be one of the smaller, more picturesque home wineries. It is still picturesque and home operated, but can hardly still be considered small. Starting with a venerable ruin of a building in 1946, the Trinchero fam-ily has patiently built it up, year by year replacing old cooperage with the most modern stainless steel fermen-tors and oaken tanks. Today they have a functional win-ery that is an intriguing blend of the latest equipment cheek by jowl with some that would qualify for space in a wine museum, but which nevertheless fulfills its func-tion. The winery is still family owned, but the days when the winery's output was such that most of the work could be done by the family members are now a rapidly fading, though unlamented, memory.

Starting in the mid 1970s, Bob's fascination with Zinfandel, which has always been one of his favorite varieties, led him to experiment with this already well established grape. The result was White Zinfandel, first introduced in 1976, which rapidly became Sutter

Above: The Wine Library at Charles Krug Winery contains sam-ples of the firm's best wines, dating back to 1943. Here, Peter Mondavi examines a fine old 1947-vintage Cabernet that is prac-tically priceless. *Right:* This ninety-foot tunnel, painstakingly hacked out of the sandstone by Chinese labor, today houses the fine wines of Spring Mountain Winery. The caves maintain a year round 58° F temperature — perfect for aging or storing wines.

Home's specialty. The demand was such that the winery has been forced to acquire larger facilities and even vineyards outside the Valley to meet a demand that in 1984 exceeded 600,000 cases. The days of Sutter Home as a quaint little winery are rapidly going by the wayside, but the emphasis is still on producing the best Zinfandel in the Valley.

Across the street and down the road a way is a small tasting room that represents only the tip of a good-sized iceberg. The sign says "Heitz Cellars"; and many people, knowing that Heitz Cellars is a comparatively small winery, assume that this is it. In fact it was until 1964, when Joe and his hardworking wife, Alice, bought the splendid old Rossi winery in Spring Valley which is the present site of their operations. The tasting room may be small, but this small salesroom moves wine at a rate totally disproportionate to its small size.

At Galleron Road is the very modern Franciscan Winery which has a capacity of over 100,000 cases a year. The interior of this winery has bank after bank of stainless steel fermentors, a very advanced and rapid bottling line, and new oaken cooperage that rates with the finest in the Valley. One of the comparatively new ventures in the Valley, it is representative of the modern ideas that are causing considerable changes in a very ancient art.

Across the Valley on Taplin Road, Joseph Phelps, who came to the Valley from the construction business, has built a winery that is a Valley showplace and an outstanding new addition to the list of fine wineries already here. Liberally endowed with the very finest of equipment including rectangular fiberglass tanks that are new to this Valley, the winery evokes much comment for the beauty of its architecture and the daring, innovative concepts epitomized in the building. Redwood salvaged from a hundred-year-old bridge has been recycled and used as wall decorations for meeting rooms that set new standards of opulence and subdued good taste. The owner evidently has already absorbed much of the Valley's feeling, for these beautiful rooms are open to the use of any qualified group.

The redwood winery occupies a knoll on what used to be the old Connolly Ranch, a cattle raising enterprise of some considerable size. There are 120 acres of vineyards within sight of the winery, which furnish the grapes for the firm's estate bottlings. In the meantime, this winery will be a fine customer for any vineyardist who can meet the wine maker's admittedly high standards.

Hidden away at the head of Taplin Road in a beautifully wooded hollow called Spring Valley, Joe Heitz crushes, ferments and ages the wines that have made him the most talked about wine maker since Andre Tchelistcheff, under whom Joe once worked. There are many beautiful old wine cellars in the Napa Valley, but Heitz Cellars is unique. The Italian who built it probably knew very little about architecture, but he had an innate love of beauty that expressed itself in a rhyolite stone building that is so perfectly proportioned, so well adapted to its purpose, that it could hardly be surpassed today, even with all the conveniences modern science has provided us. The old building serves as an aging cellar now, and handsome, well-cared-for oaken casks hold the priceless Cabernets and Chardonnays that have made Joe Heitz internationally famous as probably the best wine maker in America today... a statement which

Above: Downtown St. Helena is an interesting blend of old and new. Note the stone construction of the old Masonic Hall. Larger rocks were used on the lower levels, smaller ones higher up. The local story contends that the scaffolding was pretty wobbly as it got higher, so it wasn't trusted with the weight of large stones. *Right:* A cellarman washes down fiberglass tanks at the Joseph Phelps winery on Taplin Road. These tanks, made in Germany, are comparatively new to the Valley, but are now popular since they are eminently practical.

he vigorously denies. "Best," he points out, is a relative statement and depends on many factors, most of them variable and a matter of personal opinion. Nevertheless, he consistently turns out magnificent wines and was the leader in the movement that took Napa Valley wines out of the low or medium priced level to the higher priced status that their quality deserves and presently enjoys. It comes as some surprise to visitors that his small modern winery, housed in a hexagonal structure completed in 1972, can turn out — with equipment no different from anyone else's — wines that consistently come in at, or near, the top of the list in tastings that include the world's most prestigious and much better known wines.

Many firms, located some miles from St. Helena, nevertheless call this town home. Up on Pritchard Hill, on a site of breathtaking beauty, Donn Chappellet has built a distinctively different winery overlooking Lake Hennessey and much of the Napa Valley. Farther up the road, Jim Nichelini's winery, dating back to the turn of the century, is the scene of weekend tastings that live on in story for years. While these people do not live within the city limits of St. Helena, they nevertheless feel they are part of the community and proudly claim the town as their own.

The varied background of the town is evident in its architecture, ranging from the cut-stone buildings of the 1880s to California modern. There is a white needle-steepled Presbyterian church that is right out of New England, and a handsome, solidly built stone Catholic church that would be right at home in some affluent French wine country town. The Rhine House is blatantly Germanic, and in the sturdy, if somewhat narrow, stone bridges that cross the Napa River, the influence of the Chinese laborers who built so many of the old buildings in St. Helena shows conspicuously. The old Italian cemetery is a vicarious trip to Tuscany, and almost everywhere, the Spanish heritage of this part of California is on full display. A casual ride through the streets of the town may lead to a home of obvious luxury, or take you by rows of modest homes that are nevertheless someone's well-kept pride and joy.

The street lights along Main Street are probably as good a key to St. Helena's character as there is. Called "electroliers," these are cast iron relics of the 1915 Pan Pacific Exposition, and by modern lighting standards are painfully inefficient. They are also graceful, aesthetically pleasing, and blend beautifully with the general feeling of a town where a high efficiency sodium vapor lamp would be a jarringly false note.

Fortunately, the majority of its inhabitants recognize the values that make St. Helena so pleasant and are militantly determined to preserve them — with the people recently arrived in town leading the fray. A recent survey showed that the town's undeniable charm was "very fragile" and susceptible to damage by even minor changes. For that reason, it gives the impression of being a place where time has somehow been arrested. More likely than not, that is exactly the reason why it is different . . . and desirable.

St. Helenans know a good thing when they experience it. They energetically make sure that their children will someday be able to enjoy the values that make this little town such a wonderful place to live. They also enjoy it from day to day — and in so doing, count their manifold blessings.

Above: The Franciscan Winery boasts a very impressive array of stainless steel fermentors. This new look in wineries, replaces the older redwood tanks. *Right:* In 1883, Frederic Beringer commissioned a replica of his ancestral home in Mainz, Germany, to be erected in St. Helena. Beautifully restored, today it houses the tasting room and executive offices of Beringer Vineyards. *Overleaf:* On a knoll that is part of what formerly was the Connolly Ranch, the Joseph Phelps winery sits comfortably amidst its vineyards. Built in 1973-74, this winery is a Valley showplace.

CHAPTER III

THAT RUTHERFORD DUST

The story is told that when Andrew Tchelistcheff, the legendary wine maker of Beaulieu Vineyards, was asked what the critical ingredient was in his outstanding Cabernets, he answered, "Cabernets need a touch of that Rutherford dust." Tchelistcheff undoubtedly knew; he fermented some of the noblest wines ever produced in the Napa Valley, and people trained by him are carrying on that tradition, all with the aid of that Rutherford dust.

It is an undeniable fact that the Rutherford area imparts a distinctly different flavor to Cabernets—or for that matter, to any of the grapes grown in this region; for while the red wines have built the region's reputation, the area also produces outstanding whites, all with that distinctive something the French call *gout de terre* (taste of the earth). There are knowledgeable tasters in the Valley who can pinpoint to within a hundred yards the place that produced the wine they are tasting. Apparently the geologic makeup of the Rutherford area is so distinctive and outstanding that its characteristics are imparted so emphatically to a wine that the trained palate can pick it out unerringly. It is only fair to point out that the Napa Valley has many extremely well trained palates, so don't bet against these individuals. You'd lose, as I did.

Whitehall Lane Winery is a good example. Owned by two brothers, one a noted plastic surgeon and the other an equally noted architect, it is a modern, compact, extremely well-designed building dedicated to the making of wines which fully exploit the outstanding characteristics of its surrounding vineyards. Alan Steen, while never completely forsaking the surgical practice that brought him renown, had always wanted to be a wine maker, as had his architect brother, Art Finkelstein. For three years, the brothers searched for a spot which would fulfill their dreams. They found it in Napa Valley, in Rutherford, beside Highway 29. On a 36-acre plot, mostly planted to Chardonnay, Cabernet, Chenin Blanc and Sauvignon Blanc, they happily turn out wines that every year win awards and a host of devoted followers.

A bit farther down the road, Bernard and Evelyn Skoda found their own personal Shangri-La in a eucalyptus grove set back 800 feet from the highway. Bernard, who spent many years with Louis Martini in an administrative position, decided at an age when most men would be considering retirement that the Rutherford area was the best wine country in California. Here he would fulfill his long-held dream: he simply wanted to make the best Reislings and Cabernets in the Valley. He just may have succeeded, if a large and growing following of strong adherents is to be believed.

An affable, gregarious, silver-haired Alsatian who easily blends Germanic efficiency with Gallic finesse and Austrian charm, he is nevertheless an uncompromising perfectionist where wine making is concerned. Bernard and his hard-working wife, Evelyn, looked six years to find their winery site; judging from the results, it was time well spent. The dense stand of eucalyptus was thinned out to make room for the winery building, but enough of it was wisely spared to make a delightful little park where this charming couple often exemplify the

Above: Robert Mondavi is certainly one of the most influential, talented and energetic wine makers in the Napa Valley. *Right:* The Mission-style buildings of the Robert Mondavi Winery flank Highway 29, near Oakville. Spacious lawns are the scene of summer jazz concerts and provide a cool green island in a sea of vines. *Overleaf:* A feature of the deluxe wine tour offered by Wine Adventures is often a beautifully catered luncheon held in the storage caverns of Anderson Cellars. Even though it looks like a place where Dracula would spend his daytimes, it is a highly efficient storage facility for the winery's excellent champagne.

hospitality that has made a legend of the Napa Valley. The winery itself is a little gem: compact, efficient, and spotlessly clean. Just looking at it, one knows that the wines emanating from it will be superb . . . a supposition borne out by the first sip.

Bernard's Rieslings are done in the German manner, with enough sweetness to make them evocative of the wonderful wines of the Mosel and the Rhine. His Cabernets are big, robust Rutherford wines, while the limited amount of Moscato D'Alexandria he makes is so dainty and delicate that it is sold only at the winery. That doesn't seem to pose even a slight deterrent; people have driven all the way from Los Angeles and beyond, just to acquire one bottle — and adjudged the time and effort very well spent.

The Napa Valley has long been known as a region abounding in overachievers, but even on this fast track Miljenko "Mike" Grgich is in a class by himself. A mischievous-looking elf of a man, he was born into a large family of wine makers in Croatia, but happily traded that environment for the more productive charms of the Napa Valley, where his skill as a wine maker in all classes of wine, but especially in whites, soon earned him a large and devoted following. His fame sprang largely from the delicate Rieslings and superb Chardonnays he produced at Chateau Montelena, but an equally vociferous coterie claimed his Cabernets alone would earn him an enviable position among the best wine makers in the Valley.

Since Mike was interested in producing several varieties, he naturally gravitated to the Rutherford area where the multiplicity of microclimates made this possible. Today, in partnership with Austin Hills, he happily presides over Grgich Hills Cellar, his own winery and vineyards by the side of Highway 29 — still making superb Chardonnay and gladdening the heart of anyone who is fortunate or smart enough to taste his wines or meet him.

In each instance, the choice of the Rutherford area was dictated by its versatility. It is true that magnificent Cabernets are grown here, but it is also home to equally majestic Chardonnays, Rieslings, and Souvignon Blancs. The alluvial fans deposited in the Valley from the surrounding mountains are so varied in their mineral content and growing abilities that one vineyard may contain all four varieties, and sometimes more than one in the same row of vines. Over a period of years, the microclimates have been so well defined that the pragmatic vineyardist, eager to exploit the very best characteristics of the vineyard, plants whatever thrives best wherever that may be. On the Oakville Grade Road, in an area planted mostly to Cabernets and Chardonnays, Charles Krug has a small vineyard growing the much sought after Moscato Canelli from which a sweet dessert wine is made that is always in short supply. It is there simply because this small plot has the particular characteristics necessary to grow this particular grape; if it grew Cabernet better, that's what would be planted there.

The Rutherford-Oakville area, geologically similar, is home to Inglenook Winery — built in 1884 by Gustave Niebaum, a Finnish sea captain turned viticulturist, and Beaulieu Vineyards — which traces its beginning to 1900 when Georges de Latour, a young Frenchman with a love of beauty and wine, picked a beautiful spot (*Beau lieu* in French) in the Valley for his home and vineyards. The

Above: Small oak cooperage of 55-gallon capacity are stacked in tiers of thousands. These hold the wine which Robert Mondavi Winery carefully ages until it has acquired just the right amount of oak flavor. *Right:* Inglenook Winery, built by Captain Gustave Niebaum, still operates today. This beautiful building survived the great San Francisco earthquake of 1906 and the economic trauma of Prohibition, keeping intact the tradition of excellence the winery has enjoyed since its founding in 1884.

gracious mansions they built as neighbors as well as friendly competitors still stand and add considerably to the Valley's social charm.

The de Latour home was placed at the end of a mile-long lane of flowering trees and featured extensive formal gardens. Like many of the early figures in the Napa Valley wine scene, Georges de Latour was a cultured man, a splendid host, equally at home with a corporation president or a vineyard worker. He lived the good life of the Napa Valley to the full. He felt personally involved with every bottle of wine that left his winery, which is probably the reason that, during his own lifetime, he saw the name "Beaulieu" become synonymous with quality.

The Beaulieu Winery in Rutherford has recently been expanded by Heublein Inc., its owner. A handsome reception center serves as tasting room and shows an outstanding audio-visual report on the firm's wines. Rutherford Square, an adjacent enterprise that tastefully blends outdoor art with outdoor dining, adds considerable charm to an already charming spot.

Beaulieu Vineyards and Inglenook are both owned by Heublein Inc. but function as separate entities and are strongly competitive. The original Inglenook Winery was, and still is, a Valley showplace. A long stone building with Georgian and Gothic overtones, it nestles at the bottom of the western foothills, as solid as the day it was built. The 1906 earthquake demolished many of the Valley's stone wineries, but Inglenook's vaulted stone cellars came through the catastrophic quake with only minor damage and still can be admired today as perfect examples of how well the Valley's craftsmen built with stone. Inglenook's classic wines are aged in well preserved oaken cooperage which also serve as a stellar tourist attraction. A feature of the noble old winery is the Captain's Room, panelled in fine woods and lighted by stained glass windows, where Captain Niebaum's personally acquired drinking glasses and other artifacts are on display. Having a glass of good Inglenook wine in the Captain's Room is the supreme accolade a visitor to the old cellars can receive, a privilege very rarely granted, but always gratefully accepted.

Heublein was well aware of the value of the Inglenook and Beaulieu names, for these two wineries have always stood for the very highest quality — a fact which has been affirmed by many gold medals received in competition with the world's most prestigious wines. The present line of wines, while offering a varied price range, does not neglect the very best. It is still possible to get Beaulieu and Inglenook reflecting the high ideals instituted by their distinguished founders.

A short way down the road is the Robert Mondavi Winery, completely surrounded by vineyards. Vaguely reminiscent of the Franciscan era of California architecture, it is actually an ultra modern, highly functional building crammed with the very latest centrifuges and traditional oak barrels. Probably better than any other winery in California, this one exemplifies a perfect marriage of modern technology and sound wine making principles; Robert Mondavi will be the first to tell you that this is exactly what he had in mind when he founded his business in 1966. A dynamic man exuding a restless energy, he has probably done as much as anyone to promote the virtues of California wine in general, and Napa Valley wine in particular. His elder son, Michael, is president of the firm and also a highly

Above: Large redwood tanks, which impart no particular flavor to wine, are usually used for storage and aging of wines. These examples are at the Louis Martini Winery in St. Helena. *Right:* Perched high on the roof of an old stable, a flicker surveys the lacework pattern he and his kind have produced. Acorns will be placed in those holes, and a few days later, the flicker will listen for noise coming from the acorns. Those are the ones he will peck open to get at the insect larvae living inside.

competent enologist who has inherited his father's drive and discriminating palate, qualities he shares with his younger brother, Tim, a graduate of the University of California at Davis.

There is a popular misconception, usually fostered by wine writers enamoured of small family owned wineries, that great wine can be made only in small quantities in quaint little stone cellars with a few old barrels and an antiquated basket press. This, of course, is nonsense, and no place refutes this fable more than the Robert Mondavi Winery. It is true that at his Oakville operation every help that modern technology has evolved is employed, but basically, this is only an improvement on the methods that have stood the test of time. Robert Mondavi is a firm believer in letting wine make itself — naturally — with only a little intelligent help here and there whenever the result is a better, more natural wine. For instance, this winery was the first to make extensive use of small oak cooperage, a practice now common in the industry. Everywhere, the emphasis is on making superlatively good wine even better, and no method, whether ultra modern or traditional, is ignored if it will achieve that end.

A good example of this willingness to constantly seek improvement in wine making is the recently launched Opus I, a joint venture of Robert Mondavi Winery and Chateau Mouton headed by Baron Phillippe de Rothschild. Under the terms of this agreement, a wine using Napa Valley grapes and facilities will be vinted under the joint supervision of wine makers from both the prestigious French and American firms, with the idea of combining American technology with French finesse and tradition. Apparently the idea has considerable merit; the first case produced under this joint venture was sold for a record-breaking $24,000 at the Napa Valley Wine auction.

Georges de Latour and Captain Niebaum chose their winery sites primarily because of the grapes that could be grown there. Another man built here simply because of the beauty in which this region abounds. On a wooded knoll at the foot of the western mountains, David Doak, a millionaire industrialist, poured millions into a brick and marble Georgian mansion. Shrubs, statuary, and formal gardens made it the most grandiose setting in the Valley, but in spite of the millions spent on it, the Doak family found mostly tragedy there. It was finally acquired by Discalced Carmelites, who built a beautifully vaulted chapel on one end of the building and transformed it into a monastery.

Now, silent, contemplative men walk in the beautiful gardens; a place built for a millionaire's pleasure has finally found peace in the hands of men vowed to proverty and silence. The chapel, open to the public, offers a cool serene solace that is always appreciated, especially on a hot summer day.

The eastern edge of the Valley, especially near the Silverado Trail, is crowned by a series of rocky knolls of volcanic origin. In spite of difficulties attendant to building on such a plot, these are favored building sites and are crowned by homes generally built by people to whom expense is only a minor consideration.

All around them the vineyards spread their rows, seasonably green and gold. The Valley will not be denied; it is fulfilling its destiny and growing its grapes to gladden the hearts of men.

Above: The Captain's Room at Inglenook contains many artifacts personally used by Gustav Niebaum, who founded the winery. Here, by the light of a stained glass window, Dennis Fife examines a fine Cabernet. *Right:* In the cavernous depths of Inglenook Winery, huge old oaken cooperage hold a treasure of aging wines. These casks were assembled by skilled German craftsmen when the winery was built in 1884 and to this day age the noble wines of Inglenook. The stone ceiling, painstakingly cut stone by stone, was fitted so beautifully these cellars suffered only very minor damage in the catastrophic 1906 quake.

Above: The Vineyard Room at Robert Mondavi Winery is in constant use as an art gallery where contemporary artists can give their work a wide exposure. This facility serves thousands of people every year and is a Valley social center. *Right:* At United Vintners, a bank of stainless steel fermentors flank the more traditional oaken casks. In the foreground is a filtering unit used to free wine of suspended material.

CHAPTER IV

WHERE IT ALL BEGAN — YOUNTVILLE

Although Yountville is approximately at the halfway point in the Napa Valley measured from Calistoga to San Pablo Bay, there were many people, especially in the Upper Valley, who considered it the southern edge of the Napa Wine Country. This statement was icily denied by the many vineyardists who tended flourishing tracts south of Yountville, and who were undeniably in the Napa Valley. It also seemed an absurd statement to the growers in the Carneros region who raised many of the grapes on which the Napa Valley built its reputation. There are also wineries at Carneros Creek and several in Napa, to say nothing of the vast plantings in the hills above the town. These are all a part of the complex that makes up the entity known as the Napa Wine Country.

There was, however, some justification for the feeling that Yountville somehow had its mind on something other than wine, in direct contrast to those towns to the north where the emphasis was completely on things vinous. Yountville seemed to be more preoccupied with its restored old buildings, its veterans' hospital and the tourist trade, than it was with the industry which had its founding here. There was really nothing wrong with this, for Yountville prospered mightily on these well-springs of its affluence. It did, however, add a certain touch of authenticity to the claim that the wine country proper began just north of city limits.

While its inclusion in the wine country proper might have been slightly debatable, there was no question at all about Yountville being an integral part of the over-all entity known as the Napa Valley, and a highly interesting, picturesque one at that. It was here that the pioneer George Yount built his mill and blockhouse, and here that the first grapes in the Napa Valley were planted. The whole Napa Valley story, as far as white occupancy is concerned, began here, and its contributions to the Valley, past and present, are too substantial to be either denied or denigrated.

Although the center of wine production had unquestionably shifted northward, it was not always thus. In 1870 Gottlieb Groezinger built a substantial brick winery in Yountville, and several smaller stone wineries flourished in the area. Yountville was a wine center, and the largest town in the North Valley. Its substantial brick and stone buildings show that it was an established center of commerce when St. Helena was just a scattered village. But while the northern part of the Valley grew and prospered, Yountville remained static. A large California State veterans' hospital situated to the west of town became the main focus of interest, and the town began to get that run-down look that always seems to accrue to communities that have lived their span of life.

Then the miracle happened, and Yountville began its second lease on life. The old Groezinger winery, scheduled for demolition, was bought by a group of investors who shrewdly guessed that it could be transformed into a stellar tourist attraction — and Vintage 1870 came into existence. The old brick winery's exterior was sandblasted; and the interior, kept as much as possible in its original shape, was transformed into a delightful maze of shops, restaurants, and boutiques. There is even a well attended playhouse.

Above: Since 1873, the Magnolia Hotel has been part of the Yountville scene. Recently renovated, it boasts four small but beautifully appointed rooms, a one entree menu — and a two weeks' waiting list! *Right:* Under a cloudy spring sky, mustard blankets a field near the Yountville Crossroads and the Silverado Trail. *Overleaf:* At summer's end, a vineyard near Lodi Lane drowses in the late afternoon sun.

Yountville has become a tourist mecca, in its own right worth a trip from the metropolitan centers of San Francisco and Oakland. The charmingly restored old stone Magnolia Hotel features a one-entree meal, four diminutive rooms...and a two weeks' waiting list!

Yountville lies in a transitional zone just about at the dividing line between the Maritime Zone, strongly influenced by the fogs emanating from San Pablo Bay, and the warmer Coastal Zone which extends approximately to St. Helena. It is thus better suited to the Pinot Noir variety of red grape rather than the Cabernet which thrives on more heat, and many of the distinguished Pinot Noir vintages of the Valley originate in this area. It also grows a distinctive White Riesling, the source of some of the Valley's most distinguished Johannisberg Rieslings. As in all the rest of the Valley, the geological composition of the soil varies from place to place, so a 100-acre plot can easily be planted to three different varieties, each one occupying the place most suited to its development. This geological difference is not only detectable on the ground by soil analysis, but is actually visible from the air. The alluvial fans can be seen as variously shaded deposits, each with its own growing characteristics. Little by little, these deposits are being pinpointed and identified, so the best possible use may be made of their peculiar virtues.

It should be remembered that it took centuries of trial and error to correctly identify those places in French vineyards that would produce the ultimate grape. The process is less than one hundred years old in the Napa Valley, and while applied technology is an extremely valuable tool, the ultimate test is still the quality of the wine that is actually produced from that plot. That takes time, sometimes even generations. Some sites in the Napa Valley have been planted to three or more varieties, and the search still goes on to find the variety that will produce supreme quality in any one spot.

The veterans' hospital at Yountville, a facility of the State of California, has had a stabilizing effect on the economy of the town, since it is always there, in good times as well as bad. It is actually a self-contained town, but, as in all such establishments (even one as beautifully situated and equipped as this one), there is always a desire to get away. So downtown Yountville has a preponderance of cross streets marked "Veterans' Crossing" used by single men.

Today Yountville is a hive of activity and is definitely in the Wine Country, for one of the more dramatic changes that has taken place in the decade between 1975 and 1985 is the explosive growth southward of the viticultural scene. Vineyards now begin at the Napa city line and extend northward in an unbroken phalanx, and there is an abundance of bed-and-breakfast houses catering to the ever increasing hordes of tourists pouring into the Napa Valley. Yountville can boast a dozen excellent restaurants, and Highway 29 is bordered with new and thriving wineries.

Some of these wineries are of more than casual interest. Crowning a rocky knoll just north of the Yount Mill Road, Robert Pepi has built a substantial stone winery that looks as though it might have been built at the turn of the century, during the heyday of the Napa Valley winery building period. Actually, it was built at the end of the modern heyday of building activities in the 1970s, when the Valley experienced the most spectacular

Above: Half the fun of buying a bottle of wine is talking about it. Here at Groezingers, in the Vintage 1870 complex at Yountville, one finds an ideal setting for such conversation. *Right:* In a quiet cemetery in Yountville, a marble memorial marks the grave of George C. Yount, the Napa Valley pioneer settler. Within sight is a more appropriate living memorial — the vineyards he planted, which first demonstrated to the world the qualities that were to make the Valley world famous as a winegrowing region. *Overleaf:* Autumn brings a blaze of color to the Valley. Here, a Petite Sirrah vine glows with the last flush of autumn.

growth it had achieved since the days of Sam Brannan. With a small, dedicated and well trained staff, this medium sized winery is turning out superb wine that fully exploits the characteristics of the grapes grown in its adjacent vineyards, which are some of the best in the Valley. All the wines are excellent, but to me the Sauvignon Blanc and Semillon are exceptional.

Probably the biggest change in Yountville's enological situation took place in the mid 1970s when Domaine Chandon was established. Even the chauvinistic French, by this time, had to admit that the Napa Valley was growing grapes and making wine that seriously questioned their heretofore unchallenged preeminence. With characteristic French pragmatism, they figured "If you can't lick them, join them," so Moet Hennessey, the gigantic French champagne maker, invested millions in choice sections of Valley lands, and a sparkling new winery and restaurant were erected.

The winery is "state of the art" with all the latest innovations American technology can provide, but the heart of the system is still the méthode champenoise where the secondary fermentation that imparts the sparkle to the wine is done in individual bottles, a method little changed from the days of Dom Perignon.

There are other French touches. For instance, the product is never called "champagne," although to the American public all the criteria of that beverage are met. To the French, it lacks one vital qualification: it was not produced in the Champagne District of France. So it is dutifully labeled "sparkling wine," even though in a blind champagne tasting it probably would hold its own with the most prestigious French growths.

Domaine Chandon has acquired over 1,200 acres of Valley vineyards, mostly planted to Chardonnay and Pinot Noir. With the huge demand for grapes needed to feed its capacity of 500,000 cases yearly, it has definitely had an economic impact on the Napa and Carneros regions, and spurred the planting of the noble but often fickle Pinot Noir. While good Pinot Noir can undoubtedly be grown anywhere in the Napa Valley, those grapes would be sold to some other vintner; Domaine Chandon is not interested in anything grown north of Yountville.

A definite contribution to the good life in the Napa Valley came with Domaine Chandon's French restaurant. An integral part of the winery, it exemplifies the French tradition that good food and wine complement each other and in fact are inseparable. With an imaginative and varied menu, it set culinary standards in the Valley not only as a region of superlatively good wines but also of equally good food.

Yountville may not be as completely wine oriented as are the towns in the northern part of the Valley, but it is inevitably influenced by the vineyards and wineries at its doorstep. All the restaurants have a good wine list, and expert wine tasters abound. Many of the people who work in the Oakville-Rutherford, and even St. Helena, areas live in Yountville, finding there a way of life that suits them completely.

Evidently, the charm that made George Yount perfectly content to live out his days in this spot still works. To several thousand perfectly contented people this is the most beautiful spot in California — their joy, their pride, their home.

❧

Above: A festive setting — a holiday turkey and a bottle of good Napa Valley wine to complement it await the celebrants' arrival. *Right:* Near Yountville, a hundred-year-old Victorian mansion sits in a sea of yellow mustard — a sure sign of spring in the Valley.

Above: The Lincoln house, one of the oldest pioneer homes in the Valley, sits comfortably in the midst of its vineyards. Over a hundred years old and charmingly furnished with period furniture, the house has been used for movie and television settings. *Right:* Dating back to 1895, the buildings of Freemark Abbey contain not only the winery of that name, but also a restaurant, gift shop, and nationally famous candle factory.

CHAPTER V

BROTHER TIM'S VINEYARD

Any region that is so different that it produces its own characteristic way of life is bound to have people who epitomize that style. The Napa Valley is no exception. However, its style of life is so complex and varied, depending on who lives it, that it would be practically impossible to pick out any one person and say, "This person represents the best in the Napa Valley."

Any such contest would most likely narrow down to two, or at most three, contestants. One of these would certainly be Brother Timothy, F.S.C., the legendary cellarmaster of The Christian Brothers.

It comes as quite a surprise to many people to find that there really is a Brother Timothy, and that he actually is the boss of wine operations at The Christian Brothers. Make no mistake about it; Brother Tim is very much alive and well in the hills above Napa Valley. While he may belittle his own importance and point out that he has a superior whose orders he follows, nevertheless, his views have a habit of becoming company policy. The facts are that under his aegis The Christian Brothers have become the largest producers in the Napa Valley and the wines he ferments have acquired an enviable reputation for consistent quality. These speak for the validity of this kindly man's judgment and ability.

The Christian Brothers are a worldwide teaching order of the Roman Catholic Church founded in 1680 in Rheims, France, by St. Jean Baptiste de La Salle. It is an order of laymen who have taken vows of poverty, chastity, and obedience. Although primarily a teaching order, they made wine in their former location in Martinez, California. In 1930 during the Depression, they moved their operation to a wooded hillside on Redwood Road eight miles above Napa, where in 1903 Theo Gier had built a substantial stone winery. This location became the hub not only of their wine making operations, but also of their novitiate and boarding school. The beautiful hillside vineyards were expanded and replanted, and The Brothers began to quietly build up a following for their wine.

The success of any business venture is largely predicated on having the right man take charge at the right time. And in Brother John, F.S.C., who headed the venture until his death in 1962, The Brothers found the right man. Brother John was an extremely astute businessman with an uncanny ability when it came to picking people to work with him. Not the least of his appointments was that of Brother Timothy, who has been involved in the wine operations since 1935.

"That's quite a time to work for the same outfit without a raise!" he'll tell you with a twinkle in his hazel eyes.

The Brothers' operations soon outgrew the Mont La Salle location, so in 1950 they acquired the Greystone Cellars on the northern outskirts of St. Helena. For many years it served as an aging cellar for The Brothers' extensive stock of wines and also as a production and bottling facility for their excellent Charmat process champagne. Years and the constant beat of tourists' feet have taken their toll, until in 1984 the building was declared unsafe, and an extensive restoration program began. Many of the operations formerly carried on at Greystone were moved to The Brothers' modern installa-

Above: These two corkscrews from Brother Timothy's collection are Prohibition era caricatures of Senator Volstead, nicknamed "Old Snifter." The Senator was, understandably, not exactly popular in the Napa Valley. *Right:* The man and his lifework are epitomized in this picture of Brother Timothy, F.S.C., the cellarmaster of The Christian Brothers. The buildings of Mont La Salle are shown in the background.

tion on the southern edge of St. Helena. There they have an ultra modern complex of crushers, continuous process presses and stainless steel fermentors as modern and efficient as any in the industry. This is the hub of a planned complex that will eventually perform the greater part of The Brothers' operations in the Valley, while Mont La Salle will remain an attractively situated aging cellar and novitiate.

For many years The Brothers were the only major winery in the Valley that did not produce a vintage dated varietal. It certainly was not because they didn't have the wines — their stocks are probably the most extensive in the Valley — and certainly not because they in any way denigrate the worth of vintage dated wine. It was simply a matter of fitting the product to the market. Brother Timothy explained this to me one pleasant afternoon over a very fine glass of Johannisberg Riesling.

"For many years, we have had a steady market of repeat customers who expected that whenever they bought a bottle of our wine, there would be no surprises. They knew what to expect and it was just good business for us to produce a known and desired quality. This could best be accomplished by blending, using our extensive stocks of wines to achieve a balance that would demonstrate the very best characteristics of the wines that went into that blend. We want to assure our customers that when they buy a bottle of The Christian Brothers wine, they are buying something with which they are familiar, and which they will be able to buy next year."

That certainly made sense. For many years it was the cornerstone on which The Christian Brothers' considerable prosperity solidly rested. Then, in the 1970s, the American public began to get serious about wine. The swing to lighter beverages, especially to white wine, began and soon developed a large and rapidly growing market. A public increasingly sophisticated in things vinous began to be more selective, and their tastes naturally turned toward the better varietals. The greater sophistication and intellectual curiosity of this segment of the wine buying public began to predicate a need to serve both markets — that consisting of those who wanted to see for themselves how the vintage turned out, and those who continued to rely on the wine maker-taster-blender for complexity, balance, continuity and pleasant drinkability. And so The Brothers' present marketing policy was born.

They still make their standby blends for those whose tastes are so inclined, but they also produce superb vintage-dated varietals for those who have that preference. It is simply a case of supplying whatever the market demands as long as Brother Timothy's admittedly high standards are not compromised.

The Brothers' stock of wines is very extensive, dating back to superlative vintages, and many of these find their way into the blends sold under The Christian Brothers label. Each wine is carefully evaluated, both for its strong and weak points. Then the necessary compensating wines are added, each contributing something to the whole, so that the blend is an improvement over any of its component parts. This, of course, has been standard practice with the greatest French wines for centuries, but in America the blender must work with an added dimension. He must take into consideration the tastes of some of the American public, a group not particularly sophis-

Above: The hands of Brother Timothy gently cradle a cluster of grapes before he cuts the stem. Constant vigilance is the price, not only of freedom, but also of a healthy vineyard. *Right:* The mustard of early spring paints the slopes of Mont La Salle's mountain vineyards with a splash of brilliant yellow.

116

ticated in things vinous, but who nevertheless constitute a large part of the buying public. The skill of the blender is therefore of paramount importance.

The skill of that blender is also subjected to a test far more rigorous than any the public can provide. Before a wine goes out under The Christian Brothers label, it must pass the taste-test of Brother Timothy — and that may be the toughest hurdle of all. Many people may have had a hand in the blending, but in the final analysis, the last step is still the approval of the master of the cellar, Brother Timothy. This tall, ruddy-faced, gentle man is the soul of kindness; but when it comes to wine, he is stern, with a set of standards so high and unyielding that they would be considered impractical if the results weren't so good.

Blending is done by most of the Valley's producers, but The Christian Brothers have one outstanding advantage. Their holdings are so extensive, so scattered over the Valley that they can take advantage of the very best characteristics the Valley produces. Besides that, they have the equipment, work force and aging facilities that are so essential to the production of good wine.

As large producers who must turn out an invariably good product year after year, they must see to it that the values that have filled the display cases with medals are perpetuated. It is a duty they feel is owed to their clientele, most of whom are repeat customers of many years' standing and whose loyalty is kept by supplying a product of unvariable quality and value.

The newer, more sophisticated market certainly has not been overlooked by The Brothers. The greater part of their best vineyards' product may still go to produce a superb blend, but a very significant part is carefully selected, nurtured and bottled under a varietal label. Fifty or more years of experience go into this. I can verify from firsthand experience that when one opens a bottle of wine bearing a vintage date, there is a tasting experience in store that will long be remembered and treasured. That sticker is a cachet of nobility.

One of the characteristics of Napa Valley vintners that really impresses outsiders is the spirit of friendliness and mutual help that is so evident on all sides. It's a way of life in the Napa Valley, and time after time as these instances are related, Brother Tim figures in them. It is small wonder that he is held in such high esteem by all his competitors.

"You know," one of them told me, "I always see a halo atop a bottle of The Christian Brothers wine, and I figure that halo's worth about fifty cents!"

A tour through the cool cellars of Mont La Salle is a treat any time, but especially after Brother Tim has taken you for a tour — part of it perpendicular — through his beloved vineyards. This cultured, intelligent man has a feeling for soil, for vines and for people. Nowhere is it more apparent than when he is in one of his hillside vineyards and lets his eyes roam fondly over acres of lovingly tended vines. Somehow he seems to sum up in his own person the words that formerly graced the back label of each bottle of The Christian Brothers wine: "High in the hills above the Napa Valley, The Christian Brothers practice the ancient art of the vintner, and gladden the heart of man."

Bless you, Brother. May you live forever!

Above: Brother Timothy's corkscrew collection is so famous that when he contacted a collector's group in London, they voted him to be the head man, with the title of "Right"; their reason for ascribing that title to him was "any American would rather be Right than President." *Right:* Painstakingly coopered by skilled German craftsmen, the ancient casks of Greystone to this day mellow and age the choice wines of The Christian Brothers. *Overleaf:* The slopes near Mont La Salle glow with the crimson and gold of a mountain vineyard.

Above: Brother Timothy in his favorite spot — the vineyards entrusted to his care. *Right:* The second floor of Greystone holds part of Brother Timothy's extensive collection of corkscrews, as well as a few antique basket presses (no longer in use) and old casks which very definitely are still in use. *Overleaf:* Completed in 1889, this is the world's largest stone winery. Named "Greystone," it was for many years an aging cellar for The Christian Brothers' store of fine wines and an outstanding tourist attraction. In 1983, renovations were begun to restore the building to productivity.

Left: Holy Family Church in Rutherford has served the spiritual needs of the area's numerous Roman Catholics since 1912. After Mass, people gather to talk, renew old friendships and generally make it a pleasant social occasion. *Above:* High in the mountains above the Napa Valley, on Redwood Road, the church and school buildings of Mont La Salle rise amidst the mountain vineyards that have established an enviable reputation for The Christian Brothers. *Overleaf Left:* The Cabernet Sauvignon is the noble grape from which the finest red Bordeaux wines are made. In the Napa Valley this grape is often made into a 100% varietal wine, winning praise from wine connoisseurs the world over — especially the chauvinistic but knowledgeable French wine drinkers. *Overleaf Right:* The White Riesling grape produces a fresh, fruity wine and its waxy translucence is a visual treat.

Above: The beautifully kept lawns of Charles Krug are the scenes of numerous concerts and social gatherings. This is the oldest winery in the Napa Valley, dating back to 1861. *Right:* In the spring, new vine shoots must be tied into correct growing position, a job which provides spending money for a considerable portion of the Valley's youth.

CHAPTER VI

THE LURE OF THE HILLSIDES

With most people, established habits—especially those sanctioned by centuries of tradition—are hard to break; so it was predictable that when a vineyardist arrived from the Old World, he would bring with him the ideas and habits inherited from his ancestors. Centuries of tradition and sound practice dictated that he should plant his vines on a hillside versus a plain. It had always been thus in the Old Country. Plains were reserved for food grains and truck gardens; vines would thrive on poor soil that would cause the hardiest grains to wilt.

It is true that some vines seem to produce their best fruit when planted in "poor soil." That soil may be "poor" simply because of a deficiency of minerals; it may provide too weak a diet for, say, a carrot; but it is perfectly suited to the needs of a Cabernet. Vines will also thrive in rich soil, producing heavy, beautiful clusters usually lacking the character of those produced by a vine that has experienced some suffering.

In the Napa Valley, this doesn't always hold true. The Valley floor is largely composed of alluvial fans washed down from the surrounding heights, so the level ground offers all the advantages of the minerals in the mountain terrain, plus a level place on which to work. This greatly facilitates the movement of the machinery that has so largely supplanted labor formerly done by hand.

The early European settlers sought the hills. Schramsberg's reputation for fine wine was founded on the hillside vineyards Jacob Schram so painfully wrested from the forest. His journals recall that the product of his mountain vineyards were the "superior" grapes and that he would mix their somewhat meager output with "inferior" Valley grapes only with the greatest reluctance.

All through the hills surrounding the Valley, there are remnants of old vineyards and the wineries built there to utilize their product. Many were established simply because that was the established norm. It must be admitted that there are many factors in favor of a mountainous site, some of which are still pertinent, while others have lost their relevance in the light of modern technology. Once the vines were well rooted (and that took some backbreaking water-carrying to accomplish), they thrived in well-drained soil, since the roots of an established vine easily go down ten feet for moisture. The hills generally have more spring rain than the flatlands, and drain it off faster. A rocky hillside will hold the heat of the sun for some hours after sunset, thus hastening the process of ripening. Also, as has been stated before, the mineral content of a mountainous site can give a grape a flavor and complexity that could be achieved in the Valley only if grapes were planted in soil that had been washed down from that same elevation.

The big thing in favor of a mountain vineyard, though, was simply that grapes planted at an elevation were much less susceptible to frost damage during the critical days of new vine growth. A mountain vineyard could always be counted on to produce a crop—meager, perhaps, compared to the lush yields of the Valley floor—but nevertheless consistently producing. That virtue alone makes mountain vineyards desirable; it is no wonder that the hills around the Napa Valley still boast of many actively producing units.

Above: The bladder press is the workhorse of the industry. Fermented pomace is dumped into the perforated steel cage where hydraulic pressure exerted through a polyethylene tube presses out the remaining wine. Not nearly as picturesque as the old basket press, it is much more efficient. *Right:* Donn Chappellet's mountain top winery holds many barrels of Cabernet Sauvignon in a building partly buried in the earth. This very modern, triangular-shaped building is an often copied concept.

From the standpoint of quality, the ninety acres of Jerry Draper's mountain vineyard, crowned by an authentic-looking French provincial chateau, are probably the most valuable acres in the United States. Louis Martini, who owns many hundreds of producing acres, rates his Monte Rosso vineyard as his crowning jewel.

Modern methods of frost protection have diminished the frost danger, and the advantages of a mountain vineyard are mostly offset by the disadvantages presented to mechanized farming. If a vineyardist can get a good stretch of flat land, especially on an alluvial fan washed down from the mountains, he will usually prefer that to a mountainous setting. The big problem is that such land is very limited and probably already set in grapes, thus zealously guarded by an owner aware of its value.

There is some kind of geological deposit at the 1200-foot level — starting from Diamond Mountain near Calistoga to a point seven miles north of Napa, the vicinity of Mont La Salle — that fosters premium quality grapes. This belt contains some of the best growing areas in the United States. Fans emanating from this deposit have the same characteristics and grow grapes that have solidly established the Napa Valley wines' reputation for excellence. It also accounts for the fact that the larger vineyards in the Valley are on the west side. The eastern side has a similar deposit, but it doesn't reach as high. Furthermore, since there are fewer creeks draining the eastern side, it has a much smaller alluvial fan system. Still, Rutherford Hill, Shafer, Cuvaison, Chappellet and Stag's Leap all feed from this; and Nathan Fay's excellent vineyard is dependent upon the minerals in it.

Up on Pritchard Hill on a beautiful mountain site overlooking Lake Hennessy, Donn and Molly Chappellet have taken advantage of this phenomenon and are growing some of the best grapes in the region, which they transform into superb wines in a modernistic triangular-roofed winery which is a veritable temple to Bacchus. The distinctive flavor of these wines, which has won universal acclaim, is at least in part attributable to the soil that produced the fruit — and there is no soil exactly like it anywhere else.

On the same side of the Valley up on Howell Mountain, Tom and Linda Burgess have one of the most spectacularly beautiful views in the Valley right from their living room window. It is not only a beautiful home and view; the mountainside vineyards produce a Cabernet and Zinfandel of exceptional quality, which Tom proudly bottles under the name of Burgess Cellars.

Near the top of Veeder Mountain, Bob and Noni Travers plant their vines in the crater of an extinct volcano and produce a prize-winning Chardonnay that is pure liquid gold. Farther down the mountain, Mike and Arlene Bernstein tend their newly planted Cabernets and look forward to the next harvest when the hard work they have put into their fledgling vineyard and winery will be rewarded.

Life is hard on the mountains, but it is also tremendously rewarding, paying off as it does in a set of values that could not even be appreciated by those unaccustomed to the heady atmosphere of the heights.

Above: A picker at Chateau Montelena busily picks his way through the lush Zinfandel vines. *Right:* At Burgess Cellars, the old wall dates back to the 1890s, but the cooperage is new. The vigilant cellarmaster is a young man, part of the new breed carrying on a proud tradition. *Overleaf:* The terraced slopes of Newton Vineyards were laboriously hacked out of the mountainside, but the wine grown here is worth the effort.

CHAPTER VII

DE LATOUR, MONDAVI, VALLEJO, AND HEITZ

People who have traveled extensively in Europe are usually the first to notice that in many ways the Napa Valley resembles some of the more delightful parts of that continent. The climate is reminiscent of Cote d'Or, and the oaks and occasional scattered palms in the Valley give the landscape a decidedly Mediterranean look. A Frenchman, Italian or Spaniard would feel right at home here, because there are so many things that would remind him of his native land. That may be the reason why the region's roots strike so deeply into those wine growing countries.

Something other than similarity to native climate would have to explain the reason why so many Germans immigrated to the Valley — and throve mightily there. The 1860s and 1870s saw a mild migration of Germans to the Valley. While some of them, like Charles Krug, Jacob Schram and the Beringer Brothers, grew to be respected winery owners, the majority of them left their mark in the skilled crafts they plied in their new home. Skilled German craftsmen built the Rhine House, and some of them stayed in the Valley to embellish other homes with their skills and labors. The carved oaken heads of casks and barrels in Greystone, Inglenook and Beringer's tunnels show a decidedly Germanic flair. More likely than not, they were carved by men who had learned their trade in Germany.

The Germans also brought their skill, diligence, and discipline in the making of white wine to the Valley. While the grapes grown here are more adapted to the methods common in French vineyards—and most wines are made following the guidelines laid down by French wine makers — there are distinctly Germanic touches here and there, especially in the care and finishing of the Riesling wines. The latter day emigrants from Germany and the wine makers of German origin distinctly show preferences in their methods that can easily be attributable to their Germanic forebears.

Hanns Kornell prefers the Riesling type grape — a German import — for his excellent champagne, contrasting with his good friend, Jack Davies, who favors French origin grapes. Hanns also brings to his business typically Germanic traits — hard work, attention to detail, personal integrity, and a blunt honesty that is sometimes disconcerting to those accustomed to a less direct method of address.

When Sterling Vineyards had completed their new buildings on a knoll overlooking Hanns's Larkmead Lane winery, they gave an appreciation dinner for the Valley's winery owners who had so liberally helped them during the construction of the beautiful new buildings. Although to most people the new complex looks like a Greek monastery crowning some island in the Aegean Sea, Hanns had his own opinion. When his turn came for a few comments after the well earned complimentary remarks, he said, "I vas very glad to find, coming up here, that you vere really building a vinery. From Larkmead Lane it looks like gun emplacements. That's one vay to get rid of the competition."

Another wine maker with Germanic forebears is Joe Heitz who, although he was born in Illinois, brings to the Napa Valley the same attention to detail and blunt

Above: From time immemorial, the vineyard worker has balanced loads on his head. Here a picker at Chateau Montelena heads for the gondola with another forty-pound load. *Right:* A basket press at Stony Hill Winery spurts forth the juice of the mountain grown Chardonnay, which has established a national reputation for this tiny winery. Only very small wineries, such as this one, still use basket presses, although they once were the workhorse of the industry. *Overleaf:* The Napa Valley has been called "the Great Unfenced Park." This scene is just off the Oakville Crossroads, near the Silverado Trail.

honesty that have made Hanns Kornell a legend. A tour
of the spotlessly clean Heitz Cellars and an awareness of
the methodical, precise methods he brings to his wine
making show immediately that he comes from a race that
not only values these qualities, but makes them a way of
life. Joe's appreciation of good food and wine, his generous hospitality, and his knowledge that hard work is the
key to achievement also smacks mightily of the German.
While this nationality has no monopoly on these
qualities, it has certainly made them a hallmark.

Joe makes wines of unquestioned excellence, and has
been referred to by many responsible publications as
"probably the best wine maker in the United States."
There is no question whatsoever that he would be a leading contender for that title. The wines he makes all have
a distinctly different nose and flavor that to the initiated
immediately identify their origin. Asked about this, he
simply answers, "There's a bit of me in every bottle. I
guess I just smell different."

As could be expected, the French have left their distinctive cachet on the Valley, for no region that could
produce wine like this would long escape their attention.
French grapes, French methods, French traditions inevitably attracted Frenchmen who found here conditions
so ideal for growing the grapes of their native lands that
even these usually unshakable chauvinists began to
admit that this region was a distinct challenge to their
beloved Bordeaux and Burgundy. The Frenchman's love
for the soil found fertile ground here; for this was soil
rivaling even that of the best French vineyards, and
there was no need of organic fertilizer in this virgin,
undepleted land.

The most distinctly French winery in the Napa Valley
was Beaulieu Vineyards founded in 1900 by Georges de
Latour. While he began this winery as a comparatively
poor man, the excellence of the wine he made at Beaulieu soon enabled him and his charming wife, Fernande,
to live the lives of the French seigneurs to which nature
and their heritage had inclined them. The fact that they
did this so easily in the Napa Valley indicates how European the outlook had become. The constant stream of
Europeans had completely transformed the social structure, making the Napa Valley a small transplanted part
of the European way of life — albeit with a distinctly
American accent.

Today the French influence is still very strong, evidenced by names such as Chappellet, Beaulieu,
Cuvaison, Chateau Chevalier, Domaine Chandon,
Chateau Montelena, and Clos Duval. There are several
authentically French restaurants in the Valley. The local
wine makers speak knowledgeably of French vintages
and have the better ones in their cellars. The sons of
French "vignerons" spend the summer in the Napa Valley studying local wine making methods, then return to
France in the fall taking with them as guests, the sons of
Valley wine makers. French is a good second language to
have in the Napa Valley.

A large, recently opened operation in the Napa Valley
speaks more eloquently than anything else about French
opinion of the local wines. Moet-Hennessy, the French
champagne and cognac firm, has opened a large new
plant near Yountville, feeding off 1200 acres of choice
Napa Valley hillside vineyards. They intend to market
the wines in the United States and eventually part of
them in France, although there, by law they may not be

Above: Napa Valley vintners not only drink their own and their
neighbors' wine but also have extensive cellars of the best
imported vintages. This bin is in Donn Chappellet's excellent cellar. *Right:* As would be expected from a winery that produces
such superlative wine, Joe Heitz's aging cellar is spotless. The
large table is often used for large group dinners, which are
enhanced by a touch not often found in wineries — chandeliers
which Joe rescued from an old house scheduled for demolition.

called champagne. A Frenchman investing his hard-earned francs in a foreign vineyard is paying it the supreme accolade.

Important as the German and French influences are in the Valley, they are nevertheless secondary to the Italian, which presently is the dominant way of life. The Italians were a little late getting into the Valley, but what they lost in tardiness, they made up in numbers. In the 1880s and 1890s the bulk of the new arrivals were men who had a consuming love of the soil, a lust for life, a knack for making good wine — and Italian names.

The Italians came from all sections of Italy, but the North Italians seemed to feel most at home in this Valley while the South Italians preferred the hotter San Joaquin area. Most of the smaller wineries that date from this period were built by Italians with the help of Chinese hand labor. The large number still in use proves that they built extremely well. The Italian love of the beautiful is evident in these buildings; for while they were functional, they also achieved that simple beauty which comes so naturally to these gifted people.

The Italian influence became very strong in the decade before Prohibition, although most Italian producers made a comparatively simple, strong wine, rather than the more aristocratic complex vintages of Beaulieu and Inglenook. This stemmed mostly from the Italian philosophy that wine is something that should always be consumed with food, not used primarily as a beverage. This theory got strained a bit during Prohibition, when conditions made the beverage so precious that its consumption was not always attended with all the social amenities. The Italians could not believe that such an unnatural law could last very long, so they had a tendency to hang onto their vineyards long after others had given up and planted theirs to prunes. When the national madness finally subsided, they were ready, willing and able to resume the trade they had never really forsaken.

The post Prohibition era was a time of turmoil in the Valley, with wineries springing up overnight to help slake the great thirst. Many of these made very bad wine. They either did not survive or were forced to mend their ways as the consuming public became more sophisticated and good wine became available. But some of the giants of the industry date from this period.

Another breed of wine makers with Italian sounding names also came onto the scene. Those, however, were second generation, college educated Americans, and they brought with them a new philosophy. Led by men like Louis P. Martini, Robert and Peter Mondavi, Bruno Solari and Bob Trinchero, the industry took a new twist. Gone or minimized was the jug wine of yesterday. The emphasis was to be on quality and varietal wines, where it has been and remains to this day.

Three of the large wineries in the Napa Valley — as well as numerous smaller ones — are owned by people of Italian descent. But the greater contribution Italians have made is not as tangible as brick and mortar. Rather it is their love of hard work, laughter, good food and the joy of living. The Valley lives an Italianate way of life. Great as other achievements may be, they take second place to this joyous legacy.

The Spanish influence is strong everywhere in Central and Southern California, and the Napa Valley has not escaped it. The flag of Mexico once flew over this

Above: The Cabernet Sauvignon is characterized by a loose, open cluster and a light yield. In the Napa Valley it yields a wine quite different from that produced in Bordeaux, but which has thousands of ardent devotees. *Right:* The famed Beringer caves have been refurbished and serve not only as a repository for aging wines but as a tourist attraction that draws hundreds of thousands of visitors every year.

144

territory, and those early beginnings left indelible marks in the character of the Valley. General Mario Vallejo's Mexican land grant took in most of the Valley; and George Yount, though born in North Carolina, became a Mexican citizen in order to qualify for his own grant. It was inevitable that the contiguity of California and Mexico should result in some melding of the two cultures. The results definitely show in the Valley.

One of the early showplaces of the Valley was the Parrot house, the home of Tiburcio Parrot, an aristocrat of the first water who wore his Castilian blood as a badge of honor. He and Frederic Beringer not only were fast friends, but the social arbiters of their day. The sight of Señor Parrot and his lovely wife approaching the Rhine House in their splendid carriage, complete with liveried footmen, was one of the social highlights of early St. Helena.

In the whole of the Napa Valley, the Parrot house is probably the piece of architecture best known to the American public. Although it is owned by vintner Mike Robbins and is adjacent to his Spring Mountain Winery, most Americans would say its owner is Angela Channing, the scheming, cunning owner of Falcon Crest.

All through the Valley, Mexican land grants form the basis of ownership for many famous vineyards. Although the landed aristocracy has long since been supplanted or assimilated, vestiges of their gracious way of life — their architecture, even their cooking—persist to this day and help to give a hispanic flavor to the Valley.

The first vineyard workers in the Valley were Indians, but they succumbed rather easily to the white man's diseases. In their place to fill the vacuum, came the Chinese, then later Mexicans and Spanish-Americans who quickly demonstrated a marked ability for this work. Today, a large part of the manual labor in the Valley is done by Mexican nationals — many of them admittedly in this country by virtue of a clandestine crossing of the Rio Grande — who prune the vines, trellis the canes, and harvest the grapes. The work is sometimes cold and wet, often monotonous — and during harvest, hot and demanding. Yet the work is done to a constant stream of banter and even song. An unforgettable memory for me was to hear a bronzed, stubble-faced grape cutter with a magnificent tenor voice flawlessly render Rudolfo's aria "Che gelida manina" from "La Bohème," and still manage to cut an impressive amount of grapes. I've paid good money to hear it done in a lesser manner but certainly never with more enjoyment, especially since the setting and source were so improbable.

There has been much social agitation aimed at the grape industry because of alleged exploitation of these "poor, ignorant people," mostly by earnest urban do-gooders who have never met one of these men. One of the "poor, ignorant people" I talked to spoke five languages — fluently, was studying law, and made enough money in three months of admittedly hard work to live quite comfortably the rest of the year in Mexico. He was also willing to do work that would find few takers in a nation where most of the stoop labor is considered beneath a man's dignity, and where dedication seems to mean that more money should be paid for less work, blithely ignoring the economics involved. Whatever the argument, the point is that these men were doing a hard, useful labor, and doing it with the dignity that is the hallmark of a proud people.

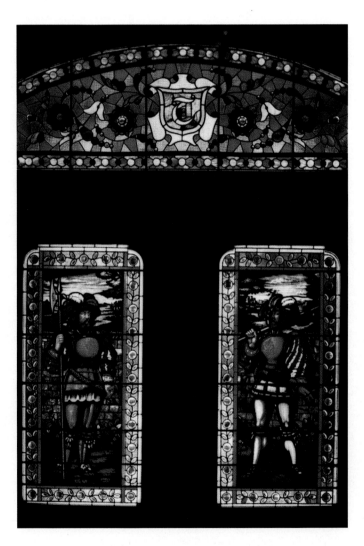

Above: In the Rhine House built for Frederic Beringer in 1883, stained glass windows enhance the Old World appearance of this beautiful old mansion. *Right:* The Old Rossi Winery, built in 1890, is now the aging cellars for Joe Heitz's fine wines. Built of perlite quarried on the property, it is a superb example of those old Italians' genius with stone.

Another ethnic group has left its indelible mark on the Valley. Everywhere, stone walls were built by clearing the land of rocks and piling them into neat rows marking the fields' boundaries. The Chinese came to California during the gold rush, which happened to coincide with a time when China was torn by an internecine feud that took twenty million lives. Often despised, persecuted, and exploited, they somehow managed to survive, leaving behind striking monuments to their genius. A people that could build the Great Wall of China may not have found much challenge in building a five-foot stone wall, but they built it with pride and expertise. They also excavated the tunnels of Beringer, Schramsberg, and Stags' Leap Winery, patiently hacking out the sandstone with pick and shovel and carrying out the detritus in baskets. Most of the stone wineries in the Valley were built with their help, and the sturdy stone bridges they erected spanning the Napa River probably will last as long as there is a need for them. Those patient, skilled, self-effacing people left their mark on the Valley, and it is a better place because they passed this way.

America has always drawn its hybrid vigor from the myriad complex of nationalities that have made this country home, and who are all, proudly, Americans, however their name may be rooted in other countries. Andre Tchelistcheff is a good American born in Russia who speaks English with a French accent and French with a Russian accent. Mike Grgich is a good American whose Croatian accent is almost as fruity as his Johannisberg Riesling. Hanns Kornell is a perfervid American whose patriotism expresses the intense appreciation and love he has for this, his adopted country. The Valley is studded with names that have their roots in France, Germany, England, Scotland, Denmark, Mexico, Holland, or almost any country you might name, each one bringing to the Valley his little touch that makes it a better place to live.

The Valley's cultural and ethnic heritage is rich and varied, a legacy of the many people who have lived here and left the best of their heritage behind. It is probably for that reason that when Michael Loesser wanted a setting for his prophetically named "The Most Happy Fella," he placed him here, in the Napa Valley.

The choice was apt. Happiness comes easily here, as a natural consequence of living in the Valley.

Above: The ranch foreman is an integral part of the system that gets the grapes off the vine and into the crusher. He is the boss— usually a man who has done every one of the jobs that he supervises. When he shows a new worker how to do a job, he speaks from a position of authority. He knows! *Right:* Bottle recycling is not a new idea, as this old rack outside the Heitz Cellars winery will attest. Back in the 1890s wine was bottled in almost any available container. This rack drained the bottles that had been washed preparatory to filling with wine.

Above: As kids will do anyplace there is water over knee deep, youngsters congregate at the popular swimming hole on the Napa River below Lodi Lane. *Right:* Young vines, trained in the manner of the Rheingau, form a pattern of living young green in the spring. Note the presence of small stones, desirable in a vineyard because it assures good drainage and a high degree of heat retention. *Overleaf:* The completely modern, automated warehouse at Inglenook Vineyards in Rutherford is computer operated. This view, taken during installation, gives some idea of its capacity. Today, these racks are full of barrels, making it impossible to repeat this photograph.

CHAPTER VIII

THE QUIET TIME — WINTER

The November rains finally come, and the newly fermented wines are consigned to their aging casks to begin the long sleep that will give them the nobility to which they were born. The fields, bereft of their harvest robes of purple and gold, stand ghostly in gray, serried ranks, the gnarled arms of the vine grotesquely reaching to the heavens in silent supplication. The winter season has come to the Napa Valley.

Although the fall rains bring a bright coat of newly sprouted grass, this is the season when there is the least apparent life in a vineyard. After their hard struggle bearing fruit, the vines rest and recoup their strength so they may produce again and keep intact nature's eternal cycle. Nutrient is stored, and although the plant goes into a state of dormancy that simulates death, it is undergoing a process that is an essential step in the complicated cycle that will produce another abundant crop next October.

Winter is the vineyardist's least busy time, but not the cellarman's. While the vineyardist waits for spring to awaken the vines so that he may again nurture them, the cellarman is busy with the last vintage. New wines must be racked; some wines must be fined and transferred from tank to tank. Vintages that have come of age must be bottled and stored, and the emptied tanks cleaned. A winery takes a lot of housecleaning, and much of it is done in winter, the quiet time.

Dormancy is an important part of the grape life cycle that produces good wine. Vintners have long known that unless a vine goes through a period of seeming death the grapes it produces will not be of premium quality. This is the reason that grapes grown in tropical climes, while they may be outwardly lush and beautiful, never seem to have the character of those grown in lands where winter imposes a breathing spell.

The Napa Valley's climate is ideal for this process, since its daytime winter temperatures hover in the 50° range, and nighttime can go down below freezing. This is fine as long as the vines are dormant. The same temperatures during the spring, when the sap has risen in the vines and the flowers have appeared, would be totally disastrous.

Winter is normally the season when the repairs and maintenance that are normal to winery care hit their peak. Fermentation tanks — especially those made of wood — must be scrubbed down, then sterilized with a burning sulphur candle. The resulting pungent sulphur dioxide gas is an active germicide that thoroughly destroys all bacteria or wild yeasts that might otherwise result in a wine of dubious quality.

Another, more dramatic operation also takes place in the winter. Right after an oaken aging tank is emptied of its contents, that tank must be rehabilitated. Sometimes, especially in a new tank, a thorough scrubbing down and sterilization will do; but in old cooperage, the tank may require a bit of drastic surgery. After many years of constant use, the wine has so thoroughly saturated a surface layer of oak that the tank no longer imparts its oaken characteristics. Instead it may carry over a flavor from a previous vintage — and that is not always desirable. In small 55-gallon cooperage this is

Above: Amidst a welter of hoses and steel fermentors, a cellarman at the Robert Mondavi Winery transfers wine from one tank to another in the complicated process that leads to superlative wine. *Right:* Near the Carmelite Monastery at the foot of the Oakville Grade, the pruned vines form a neat pattern leading to the eastern edge of the Valley. This scene is in early February.

solved by dismantling and cleaning the barrel, stave by stave, and then reassembling it. Larger oak casks, many of them holding thousands of gallons, are quite another matter. Building casks like this entails skilled labor, the best of materials, and generous amounts of money— and some or all of these may be in short supply. The fine old casks of Inglenook, Beringer and Greystone, now nearly a hundred years old, are almost completely irreplaceable as aging tanks, to say nothing of their value as art objects.

In cases of extreme deterioration, a thorough scraping of the inside surface of the tank so a new layer of oak is exposed restores the tank's characteristics. Since the chances of ruining the tank are quite high, this process is resorted to only when the cask is very valuable or in such an advanced stage of deterioration that scraping is considered the last resort. Tanks are regularly scraped to remove the tartrates that accumulate during the aging process. This, to a certain extent, helps reveal new wood and extend the useful life of a tank.

The fermentation of a new wine is an extremely active process, one that produces numerous by-products as well as the primary wine. Many of these remain suspended in the wine until a long rest settles them out, unless some artificial means to achieve this end is employed. The old time vintner let nature do the settling, a process that usually took months or years. His modern counterpart uses centrifuges or a settling process known as fining to clear the wine of suspended material and produce the crystal clear wine that American taste demands.

Fining may be done several times during the life of one vintage, or only once if the original treatment results in a suspension-free wine. The usual material used is Bentonite, a type of infusorial earth that is mixed with water into a thin slurry and added to the tank's contents. The Bentonite settles to the bottom, taking with it the suspended material and leaving the wine clean and bright. Other materials such as gelatine solutions are sometimes used for the same purpose—to rid the wine of suspended particles that do not particularly harm it, but certainly detract from its aesthetic appeal. There is considerable difference of opinion as to whether or not this detracts from the quality of a wine. Most vintners feel that it does not; however, it immeasurably improves the appearance of a wine, thereby enhancing its acceptance by an increasingly critical public. Occasionally, a wine will "fall bright" without any outside help. This is usually gleefully bottled and labeled as such, so there may be some virtue in abstention from the process.

Winter is a busy time in a winery, with much pumping, transferral of wines, and record keeping; but the single most important operation that takes place during the winter is the blending. This is, in effect, a marriage of wines.

Most wines, even the very finest, are blends. This does not mean that there is any adulteration involved in the negative sense, since the blending is usually undertaken to add some quality that even a very fine vintage may be lacking. The Cabernets of Bordeaux, for instance, are by themselves much too astringent; but the judicious addition of carefully calculated quantities of Merlot—a soft, comparatively bland wine—results in a product that is better than either one of its component parts. The resulting combination still retains the varietal characteristics of the Cabernet Sauvignon grape.

Above: The German ovals at St. Clement Winery are not only highly efficient storing and aging vessels, but are also excellent examples of the modern cooper's art. *Right:* Inside one of Beaulieu Vineyard's huge stainless steel fermentors, a cellarman scrubs down the tank to a standard of cleanliness that would please the most meticulous housewife.

Blending, in a wine which will have a vintage year and a varietal label, is carefully controlled by law. A wine carrying a varietal name must be at least 51% of that grape and have the distinctive characteristics attributed to it. If the wine is vintage dated, it must be 95% of that year. Places of origin given on a label are also subject to regulation. If the wine label says "Napa Valley," at least 75% of the total volume of that wine must have originated there. These are all minimum requirements and, happily, are usually exceeded by most premium producers. However, since these requirements are law, they are strictly policed and enforced.

The vintner, before making a blend in quantity, makes a carefully regulated batch that has the characteristics he desires. His guideposts are experience, a knowledgeable palate and the reaction of trusted tasters. If that blend falls withing the limits imposed by the vintage bottling law, he will then mix his wine in quantity, age it and hope the whole process will result in a product he can market with pride as well as profit.

A winery with a large stock of its own wines has a distinct edge in the blending process. Not only are the characteristics of the wines thoroughly known, but since all of the components are made by one firm, they easily fall within the limits imposed by the label, which must state who made the major part of the bottle's contents. Smaller wineries must have a thorough knowledge of what their neighbor's or even competitor's tanks hold—a situation which is approached with an enthusiasm that does much to enhance the Valley's reputation for outstanding hospitality.

Winter in the Napa Valley is relatively mild, but somewhat on the dampish side making most of the outdoor work sodden misery. Most of the Valley's thirty-three inches of annual rainfall comes during the winter. It is sucked up by the soil and slowly trickles down to the roots, where it will feed the vines during the active growing periods of spring and summer.

Although some pruning is done in the fall immediately following the harvest, most of it is done in winter and early spring before the vines actively begin to grow. This is a most important step, since the yield of that vineyard is pretty much predicated on the skill with which it is done. The most vigorous spurs are selected and pruned back so only two, or at most three, buds are retained on which flowers will sprout, eventually becoming a bunch of grapes. Care must be taken to retain only a few buds so the vine can supply enough nutrient to nourish the fruit it will bear and keep a nice balance between quality and quantity. An correctly pruned vine will either produce too many grapes (overcropping) which will not ripen, or well ripened grapes in small quantity. Obviously, the optimum condition would be to have a vineyard pruned so it produces the largest possible amount of ripened grapes. For that reason, skilled pruners are very much in demand, since their judgment will directly influence the quality of next year's crop.

Winter is a season that must simply be endured if one is to taste the delights of spring. In the snug homes, however, fireplaces are lighted, old port lovingly decanted, and preparation of meals becomes a high art. New wines are tasted, new techniques disclosed, and ideas that will result in a better product next season are thoroughly discussed. The stage is being laid for the awakening.

Above: In early March the sun throws long shadows across the lawn of the Niebaum House, while in the Valley the morning mists have yet to be dissipated. *Right:* In the Vineyard Room of Robert Mondavi's Winery at Oakville, well attended classical concerts enhance the winter social season.

Above: The mists and rains of late winter and early spring may be a bit uncomfortable, but are necessary if the vines are to have the deep-down moisture which will nourish them during the hot days of summer. *Right:* Pruning is usually done in the winter, but in the mountains, where the vines become dormant very early, it can be done immediately following the harvest. Here a worker trims off a cane, leaving only the strong spur which will bear new wood for next year's crop.

CHAPTER IX

THE AWAKENING—SPRING

Almost overnight, the air acquires a certain softness; a gentle haze cradles the increasing warmth; and in the vineyards the gray vines suddenly burst forth in a fringe of delicate green that presages the activity that is to come. The winter rains have already greened the tan hills, but now the flowers burst from the soil and paint the slopes with splashes of vivid color. Down in the Valley, the almond trees explode in puffy white clouds of blossoms, and the very air is somnolent with the drone of busy bees. Spring has come to the Napa Valley, and characteristically, it has come beautifully.

Though it is a time of beauty, it also is the most dangerous time of the whole year. Frost is an ever present danger, since new vines just emerging from the deep sleep of winter can easily be killed by subfreezing temperatures. New shoots are even more susceptible. Thirty minutes of subfreezing temperatures can damage them to the extent that when the morning sun finally warms them, they wilt, blacken and die. There will be no crop this year from those particular vines.

It used to be that the only protection against this danger was to plant a vineyard on a hillside not susceptible to frost — or have an extremely good working relationship with, and faith in, the Almighty. Today, some added safeguards are available, although few people would turn their backs on the old standbys.

One of the most common questions asked by visitors to the Valley is "What is the function of the thirty-foot towers studding the vineyards?" These towers always mount an engine driving a large aircraft type windscrew and are arranged in such a pattern that a breeze can be set up that covers all parts of the vineyards. They are such an intrinsic part of the landscape that most natives take them completely for granted, as though they had grown there.

These are wind towers, the first line of defense against frost. Subfreezing air tends to be denser, and hence hugs the ground. If a breeze is set up, the warm upper air circulates over the vines and blossoms, and so helps to avert freezing. Until an awareness of air pollution made it impractical, smudge pots and orchard heaters were also used to supply that critical one degree that might spell the difference between freezing and survival. Smudging is frowned upon nowadays, but almost every orchard has a few heaters strategically located. One can always argue about the propriety of using this equipment, and the user can become extremely eloquent in its defense, especially if its use has saved his crop.

Most vineyardists rely on a most sophisticated method of frost fighting. The whole Valley is studded with water reservoirs which not only provide badly needed irrigation water during the critical growing periods up to about mid-June, but also serve as a standby frost protection system. A vineyard equipped with this system will have a frost alarm which clangs lustily in the vineyardist's bedroom if the temperature should become critical. He may choose to fight the frost by turning on a sprinkler system that immediately warms his vineyard with a fine rain of above-freezing temperature water. If the temperature is cold enough to freeze the rain, he benefits by the fact that freezing water is an exothermic process and so gives

Above: A special tractor, designed specifically for vineyard use, takes much of the back-breaking work out of tending a vineyard, but the work is still hot and demanding. *Right:* The origin of the Zinfandel grape has been the subject of much speculation, but it has become the most classically "Californian" of all wine grapes. In the Napa Valley, it reaches a perfection that challenges even the lordly Cabernet.

off heat. And lastly, the freezing process coats his tender young shoots with an insulating coat of ice, shielding them from the too-cold air. The young growth will not tolerate 30° for more than a half hour, but 32° seems to do no apparent harm. So a casing of ice, while apparently deadly, is in reality a gleaming lifesaver that can make the difference between a bearing vineyard and a zero crop.

The most highly visual sign of spring in the Valley is the coat of bright yellow mustard weed that bursts into bloom between the rows of gray-brown grapevines. The origin of this floral display reads like something out of the Hansel and Gretel story. Legend has it that when Father Altimira first visited the Napa Valley in 1823, he carried with him a bag of mustard seed which intentionally had a small hole in it. This was mounted on one of his burros in such a manner that the motion of the animal allowed a thin trickle of seeds to drop. Retracing his steps a few months later must have been relatively simple; he simply followed the ribbon of growing gold that marked his previous trail.

However it got there, mustard is in the Valley's soil to stay — especially if the vineyardist has anything to say about it, and he most assuredly does. This crop not only prevents erosion but also adds a saffron slash of color to the Valley in the spring, a not inconsiderable asset in a Valley where beauty is part of everyday life. It is also a valuable cover crop which, turned into the soil in midspring, provides a series of aquifers and a valuable shot of green fertilizer.

Spring is also the time when the various diseases that can plague a vineyard are busily attacked. Both helicopters and ground rigs are used to spread the sulphur compounds that inhibit the oidium, commonly known as powdery mildew, that must be prevented from taking over the vineyard. In mountain plantings, a constant irritant is the poison oak that seems to flourish in even the poorest soil and is always ready to add its irritating itch to the vineyardist's list of troubles.

And that list is long! There are several dozen diseases that can attack a vineyard, and while only a few of them are common or widespread, they all require surveillance and constant vigilance. As soon as the rains have abated, the vineyardist is out on his land, scrutinizing every vine with an eye trained to spot the slightest abnormality and ready to nip in the bud any disease that could affect his vineyard. Eternal vigilance is not only the price of freedom, but also of a healthy vineyard. While to the casual observer a vineyardist may seem to be simply glorying in all the beauty that surrounds him on a balmy spring day, he is really checking on all the problems that must be attended to now if he is to be happily busy in early October.

Spring is a beautiful season in the Valley, but vineyardists understandably breathe a sigh of relief when this gorgeous, but potentially dangerous, season has safely merged with summer. Disaster can come any time of the year, but spring is the time when it is most imminent. The fact that it comes disguised in robes of transcendental beauty does not detract one iota from its potential deadliness; it only emphasizes it.

Still, anyone falling under the spell of the new life, fragrant blossoms, and puffy, lazy white clouds hanging over a landscape daily revived will tell you that for all its potential danger, this is still the magic time of the year.

Above: Mustard weed is not only highly decorative in the springtime but is also a valuable cover crop. *Right:* The helicopter is an invaluable tool for spraying a sulphur solution to keep down mold in grapes almost right for the harvester's hand. In left background are the buildings of Sterling Vineyards.

Above: Spring brings rain, mist and flowering mustard. One of the many moods of the Napa Valley, it is one more aspect of a Valley that is always changing. *Right:* Grape vines live almost a hundred years, and some exceptional specimens exceed even that. This sturdy specimen, one of the original Inglenook vines, is almost eighty years old. Although this one is still producing vigorously, most vines are replanted after about forty productive years. *Overleaf:* Although die-hard environmentalists object to orchard heaters (they call them "stinkpots"), a vineyardist who has had his crop saved by these heaters can become very vociferous in their defense. Ten of these diesel burning heaters and a wind machine can raise the temperature of a vineyard three to four degrees per hour, which can mean the difference between a crop or a crop failure.

CHAPTER X

THE LONG, HOT SUMMER

By the calendar, summer arrives around the twenty-first of June, but to a vineyardist summer starts once his vines have flowered and acquired the "set" that will grow into grapes. By mid-May the vine has put forth buds which look very much like a miniature bunch of grapes, but before these can form into fruit, they must go through the flowering process. This usually happens in the first ten days of June, although hot weather can advance the date, or cold weather retard it. The pale white flowers are so small, so seemingly insignificant, that most visitors overlook them entirely. Yet without them there would be no grapes in October, for this is the birth of a cluster. Unless conditions are just right — moderately dry, warm weather — the vines will not set a full crop of fruit. The vineyardist will have acres of pretty green leaves to look at, but that's all.

If everything goes well, by late June the grape clusters are apparent and growing rapidly. Soon they will have attained the shape and number they will keep till harvest, and the vineyardist can begin to make some estimates of his crops. If it is unusually heavy, he may thin it to get optimum quality — a slow, arduous process which he does grudgingly while counting his blessings. In some varieties, he may partially defoliate his vines to allow sunshine into the interior so clusters otherwise hidden by the leaves may ripen. It means long, hard, arduous hours in the vineyards, under conditions which can best be categorized as brutal. When the Bible mentions, as the epitome of hard labor, the work of the laborers in the vineyards, the vineyardist knows what it's all about. He's been there.

Still, the work must be done, and it must be done now, if there is to be a crop later on. Summer in the Napa Valley, cooled as it is by its proximity to San Pablo Bay, is relatively mild compared to the infernoes of the inland valleys. Still, it counts several days when the mercury pushes past 100° F. This is the time when the heat needed to ripen the fruit is accumulated. It is also the time for general maintenance in the fields. Suckers must be trimmed, canes tied and trained, and pesticides applied. There is no romance in tending a vineyard during the summertime, just hard work; very often this is when a would-be vineyardist finds out if he has the stuff it takes to succeed in this game. During the long, hot summer the men get separated from the boys pretty quickly, since the blazing sun plays no favorites.

In July the tempo picks up a bit. As soon as the first blush of color appears on the grapes, equipment is readied. Tanks are washed down and sterilized, gondolas are painted, and the mechanical devices with which all wineries abound are put though a "dry run" to make sure they are ready for the frenetic months ahead. Once that is done, there is little left to do except wait for the sun and mist to work their magic on the vines, now growing increasingly heavy with their loads of swelling fruit.

Summer is the big tourist season in the Valley, in spite of the fact that vines in summer look like so many rows of dusty bushes. The twin roads that bracket the Valley carry a never-ending stream of cars that divert themselves into wineries' entrances until the parking lots are full, then keep on going till they hit the end of the Val-

Above: By early summer the grape clusters have formed, assuming the position they will hold till maturity. Careful vineyardists check the clusters for size, and if necessary, thin them, so the remaining berries will achieve maximum quality. *Right:* It is near summer's end and the grapes hang seemingly ripe on the vine. But the cool touch of fog off San Pablo Bay helps cause just the right amount of fruit acid to make Napa Valley wine so different, and so desirable.

ley and turn back. Residents of the Valley have known for years that Highway 29, on which most of the wineries front, is completely inadequate to carry the monstrous traffic loads imposed upon it. Nevertheless, if there is one single point on which the Valley stands united, it is in a fanatically firm opposition to a freeway. Valley residents feel this would not solve their problem, but only aggravate it. The bureaucrats in Sacramento have finally gotten the message; in 1974 the last parcel of land acquired years ago for a freeway was returned to the purpose for which it is best suited — growing grapes. If the residents have anything to do with it, the freeways will never come to the Napa Valley.

Most wineries conduct tours of their premises the year round (with the possible exception of a few frantic days at the height of the crush) and usually end the tours in the tasting room. It is a very hardy soul indeed who can go the length of the Valley without having added a few bottles to his cellar or pounds to his waistline—or both.

Some wineries make this source of distribution their main sales effort; others use it only as an adjunct to a regular sales program. All find it highly lucrative, while the tourist finds it thoroughly enjoyable. No wonder the system flourishes!

Summer is also the season for festivals in this Valley where the enjoyment of life takes second place only to work. Charles Krug Winery has for many years held festivals on its immaculately groomed lawns shaded by giant, several-hundred-years-old oaks. Its August Moon concerts are very high caliber, employing the very best professional talent and drawing audiences from the metropolitan centers. These concerts tend more toward the classics, and draw a sedate, pensive crowd. The grounds are also the scenes of a weekly wine tasting for selected customers and friends, where Peter Mondavi very proudly shows off the not-inconsiderable talents of his prestigious winery.

Down the road at his brother's winery, Robert Mondavi has a different kind of concert. Largely youth oriented, it features popular jazz bands and groups, which always draw capacity crowds, most through the front gates but also clandestinely through the vineyards. Again, wines are tasted, appreciated, discussed and bought. Everyone has a good time, except the harried caretakers who must pick up after a young crowd more dedicated to ecology in word than in fact.

Most of the wineries provide picnic tables or a pleasant place to open a bottle of wine — from the obvious source — to share with a lunch. The little park in the center of St. Helena does yeoman service, as does the public riverside park at Calistoga. Less well known are the Chinese pagodas at Chateau Montelena or the picnic tables at Burgess Cellars that have a view unequalled anywhere in the Valley. A little off the beaten path, but well worth seeking out, is Crane Park behind the High School in St. Helena. Well equipped with shade trees and picnic benches, it is a delightful spot.

Summer is a waiting time, a hush that comes over an audience just before the curtain rises for the main act. It is a time of preparation, of anticipation; as the swelling grapes grow lush and full in the sun, all eyes are bent toward the drama that is soon to unfold.

❧

Above: Rollie Heitz reads the degrees Balling on his saccharometer and is content. Another good Heitz vintage is in the making. *Right:* The early morning sun backlights ripe Green Hungarian grapes in the Jerry Draper vineyards on Spring Mountain.

172

Above: The Moscato Canelli grape is grown only in small quantities in the Napa Valley; here, this luscious sweet grape attains a complexity that makes the wine produced from it always in short supply. This bunch is from the Charles Krug vineyard on the Oakville Grade. *Right:* Young shoots emerge from this mature vine, which has been pruned so only its strongest spurs remain to bear fruit. The small but visible flower clusters will in time grow into a cluster of grapes.

CHAPTER XI

THE CRUSH

The warm days of July and August have done their work; on the vines the grapes hang, lush and ripe looking, seemingly ready for the hand of the picker. All the hard work that has been done all year — all the hopes and expectations — reach their culmination in late August or early September when the blush on the grape reaches its deepest hue. The time of the crush is at hand.

Vineyardists who long to see their grapes safely off the vine and into the crusher point out that the fruit has reached the ultimate state of desirability. More pragmatic wine masters, armed with refractometers, opt for those few extra days to give the grapes exactly the right balance of fruit acid and sugar that results in a superlative wine.

Finally, the day comes when all these conditions are just right, and the pickers move into the vineyards. It is the opening gun in what can best be described as a well-thought-out military campaign.

On one side are marshalled all the negative forces that can impede the making of good wine. Their weapons are wind, rain, hail, high temperatures, and fog. Their allies are flocks of voracious birds who can easily eat their own weight in grapes each day, and deer that can jump an eight-foot fence or wriggle through a hole that would present a challenge to a small boy. These graceful, beautiful and extremely destructive scavengers will eat anything the birds have missed, down to the wood of the main vine itself. Bees may not seem like much of a problem, but their voracious appetite for the juicy nectar of the grape accounts for their presence around the vineyards. Also allied against the vintner are cantankerous machines that can break down at the most inopportune time, and the ever present human errors that can negate even the best efforts. But the biggest enemy of all, and the most implacable, is time.

It takes a beautiful synchronization of events to turn a grape into wine, and every one of them is based on good timing. There is an optimum time for a grape to be picked; it must reach the crusher within a few hours in order to be crushed at the right sugar level; and the fermentation must take place within carefully defined limits of temperature. Any number of things can go wrong that will turn that beautiful load of expensive grapes into so much spoiled must, good for nothing except to fertilize a vineyard.

On the other hand, the vintner has quite a few things going in his favor; otherwise wine would be even more scarce and expensive than it is. For one thing, a ripe grape is a natural wine factory that only needs its skin broken to begin operations. Vintners will tell you that they themselves do not make wine; wine makes itself. All they do is direct it a bit here and there. Their job is to assist nature wherever their intervention will help or speed things up. Then, too, the making of wine is not the haphazard affair it was back when cavemen inadvertently squashed some grapes and so started the whole wine industry. Over the centuries, a store of knowledge has accumulated that can predict, with a certain amount of reliability, what will happen once the grapes have been consigned to the crusher. It's a good thing the vintner has a few things going for his side, because the obstacles are certainly many — and assuredly formidable.

Above: Vineyardists know that when a star pattern forms in the juice squeezed from a grape, the fruit is close to optimum ripeness and ready for the crush. *Right:* Balancing a forty-pound load isn't easy, but this young man, hurrying through the golden glory of a vineyard with his lug of Cabernet Suavignon grapes, makes it look like play.

While the rule of thumb is that grapes will be ready for picking fifty days after the first color appears, this is at best a rough approximation, especially in white grapes. Some harvests can begin as early as the last week in August, especially if the weather has been hot and dry, or linger on into November if rain and cold weather have been prevalent. Also, different vintners would pick the same vineyard at different times, depending on their sugar content requirements. Sugar content is measured with a scale method delineated by Degrees Balling, usually marked as ° B. Jack Davies will pick his Pinot Noir grapes at 19° B to make his superlative champagne, because he values fruit acid and low sugar. Robert Mondavi would prefer a 23.5° B for his Pinot Noir varietals. The usual difference is time, which allows the sugar to build up to the Mondavi requirements, while an early picking would suit Jack Davies's requirements better.

It is a very fortunate circumstance that different species of grapes ripen at different times, else the wineries would experience a few days of phenomenal glut. Even as it is, it takes a master tactician to juggle the time schedules so the right grapes arrive at the proper time. If one grower goes off schedule, it throws off all the rest — a situation which, if often repeated, is not particularly guaranteed to enhance the guilty one's popularity with his peers. As a general rule, white grapes ripen first, while the last Cabernet Sauvignons are often picked during the first rains of November.

One of the conditions that make the Napa Valley such superlatively good wine country is the fact that the weather usually cooperates with the vineyardist. This is not an absolute fact; vineyardists still remember with a shudder the drought years of 1976 and 1977. Then too, there was the premature year of 1984; the harvest actively started in mid-August and was effectively over by mid-October, a time that would have normally witnessed the height of the crush. The puzzling thing is that the drought years produced some unusual wines of distinct interest, and 1984 may well have been one of the better years in the century. This is in spite of the fact that Cabernets were reaching their optimum sugar levels at the same time as Chardonnays, and crushing operations were often carried out by the light of the moon.

While new techniques of grape picking have been introduced, the time honored method of picking the crop, cluster by cluster, still predominates. By the dawn's early light, the pickers move into the fields well bundled up against the pervasive chill of the fog, and further ward off the cold by setting a terrific pace during the cool morning hours. Later, when the sun has dissipated the mist and the heat of the day has set in, there will be time to slow down, to pace oneself so there is still enough steam left by quitting time to enjoy a social drink and some good natured banter with friends.

The crush is the time of year toward which all other efforts have been pointed. All the preparation — all the planting, cultivating, pruning and trimming — has been aimed toward this time when the fruit leaves the vine and trades one life for another. Wine is unique in that it is a living entity, with a cycle of birth, youth, maturity and death — and the cycle starts here, during crush.

Like most birth cycles, the crush is dramatic and sometimes a bit messy. After the grapes have been cut from the vines and piled into the brightly colored lug boxes, they are dumped into a gondola, which, after

Above: Joe Heitz inoculates a batch of new wine with a strain of yeast which will produce the characteristics he likes in his wine. The yeast comes from the Institut Pasteur in Paris, France, and is carefully cultured each year to produce the same predictable results. *Right:* The hands of a grape cutter — skilled, strong and knowing — support a cluster of Zinfandel grapes before the swift stroke that will separate it from the vine, sending it on its way to a new life as wine.

being weighed, is tilted by a hoist so that its contents are dumped into the crusher. A helical worm (screw) pushes, shoves and moves the fruit into the crusher, while the motion of the stemmer separates the leaves and stems from the new must. In red wines the must is pumped, in a pulpy, liquid state, to its tank where it will ferment up to six days. The pulped fruit will float on top of the solution, over which the new wine is pumped twice a day. The alcohol that is a product of fermentation dissolves the pigmentation in the skins, and gives the wine its characteristic color. Rosés are allowed to stay on the skins only long enough to pick up a little color, while whites have practically no contact with the pulp. In making white wine, the free run juice is piped directly to a fermentation tank, while the pulp is pressed immediately to get out all the rest of the juice. This is added to the free run and contributes some tannic qualities to the wine that aid it in the aging process. The juice is fermented out of contact with the pulp.

While grapes are being crushed, a measured amount of potassium metabisulphite is thrown into the must to kill any bacteria and wild yeasts that may be on the grapes. The resulting solution is then impregnated with a strain of yeast whose characteristics are well known, and the fermentation starts.

A tank of red wine in full fermentation is really a sight to behold, for the fermentation of sugar produces approximately equal parts (by weight) of alcohol and carbon dioxide. The carbon dioxide is released as bubbles, which induce a great, rolling boil in the tank, as though some submerged monster were in its death throes. The fermentation process also releases heat which must be dissipated, else the whole batch could be spoiled. This is one reason fermentation tanks in Europe were almost always in cool cellars and caves; the cool temperatures helped keep the wine tank and its contents within acceptable temperature limits. Nowadays, the heat of fermentation is controlled by jacketed tanks through which refrigerant is piped, so the modern vintner has complete control of his fermentation every step of the way. In making white wine, the degree of activity is controlled by keeping the juice just barely above that temperature point where fermentation is possible.

It is certainly a far cry from the system of only a few years ago when the method used was basically to crush the grapes, dump them in a tank, and pray. Modern vintners become quite religious during the crush, but they also have a few means of control in their own right. It is true that a grape has everything within itself needed to make wine (and it is itching to do just that), but somehow the process always seems to work much better if a little intelligent help is administered wherever it will do the most good. The secrets of the grape are being systematically unravelled, so every year we come closer and closer to the time when all the secrets will be known, and therefore can be controlled. Still, as one knowledgeable wine maker puts it, "We've come a long way in the last few years, but we still have a long way to go ere we get out of the grape everything that God created . . . but we're working at it!"

The vineyardist whose grapes are picked early is the one who can relax. Not so the man with a hundred acres of grapes whose sugar is not quite right, or who has varieties currently not much in demand. Every year some grapes may be bypassed, and hang on the vines because

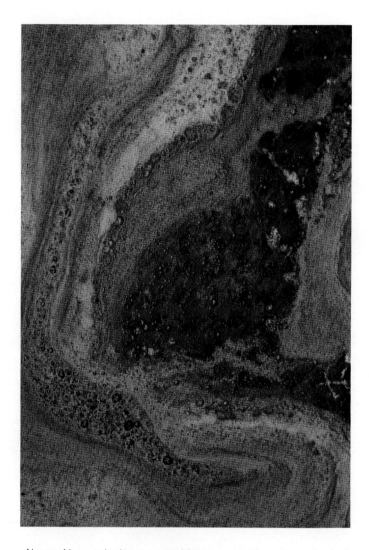

Above: New red wine pumped into a sump forms a pattern of swirls and bubbles. This new wine still contains much of the carbon dioxide which is a by-product of fermentation. *Right:* At Louis Martini Winery red wine is drawn from the bottom of the concrete fermentor vat and pumped over the cap. The alcohol in the new wine dissolves pigment in the skins, imparting to the wine its distinctive ruby tint.

there is no demand for them. It's one of the breaks of the game, and a bitter one. Fortunately, the new plantings in the Valley, now just coming into production, are all of highly sought after varieties of which there is usually a shortage. Little by little, older vineyards planted to Burger or Golden Chasselas — species much in demand years ago but now no longer in vogue — are being replaced by Cabernet Sauvignon, Pinot Noir, and Pinot Chardonnay, for which the demand seems endless, as long as there are tanks available to store the wine.

There is a special atmosphere in the Valley during the crush, an air of excitement that pervades everything. From the first pre-dawn rumble of the gondolas on their way to the fields, through the rush of the day, to the cool nights when lights glare above the still busy crushers, there is something that would let even the most blase stranger know that this is a special time. After the first week, the odor of newly fermented wine hangs like a perfume over the whole Valley, adding much to the feeling of excitement and bustle that is characteristic of the crush. This is the time of the last battle in the campaign, one that must be won if there is to be a prize.

The crush reaches its peak by the middle of September, and continues full blast for almost a month. By the middle of October, there are signs of slackening, although there is still plenty of activity in the later-maturing red wines. During this period, the whole energy of the Valley is dedicated toward the ending of the grape-growing cycle. There are few parties during this time of the year; everyone is too busy and too tired. The parties will come — with a vengeance — once the harvest is safely in the barn, the new wines are sleeping in their tanks, and the weary vintner can afford to rest from his labors. By the last of October, the end is in sight. The vintner begins cleaning up the mess he didn't have time to take care of during the harried days when he was crushing grapes. It's really what he's been working for all year. Nevertheless, when the crush is done, he heaves a sigh of relief—and feels vaguely discontented. The battle is over, and he has won, but he somehow misses the fighting. That feeling won't last too long; he has other battles to fight before his infant wines grow up to release their joy to a waiting world.

The new wines are gently bubbling in their tanks or safely sleeping in the oaken casks, and another crush, the latest in a long line going back thousands of years, has been completed. Now is the time to call a few friends, set a festive board, and taste the new wines. It will take months to properly evaluate them, for they are still children, and need much growing up. Still, a man can always call upon his friends for a pleasant task such as this one, secure in the knowledge that tomorrow it will be his neighbor's tank he is sampling and evaluating.

Many a man, in the twilight of his life, will tell you the best years he ever spent were his years in military service. Forgotten are all the bad, even hideous things, while the comaraderie, the pranks and the good times become even better in the retelling when they have achieved the patina of age. So it is with the crush. It's work, hard work; yet each year the vintner looks forward to it, perhaps with a sigh of resignation and a few complaints, yet secretly reveling in the fact that he is a man doing a man's work, and glorying in it. It was ever thus. It may very well forever be so.

🐜

Above: Meticulous record keeping is an integral part of the making of fine wine. Here, Dr. William Casey of St. Clement consults with Dennis John, his wine maker. *Right:* New wine, just a few days old, is being drawn from the bottom of the fermenting tank and run into this screened sump. From here, it will be pumped over the cap, in the process leaching out more color from the pigment in the skins. *Overleaf:* Puncturing the skin with its sharp proboscis, the bee feeds on the sweet nectar that exudes from the grape. The grapes in the foreground have already been visited by bees, and are already fermenting.

CHAPTER XII

LA DOLCE VITA

As any student of human affairs well knows, the lives and characters of a people are definitely influenced by the environment in which they live. The fabled islands of Polynesia produce a cheerful, happy people, a reflection of the earthly paradise in which they live; while the craggy islands of the North Atlantic rear a people strong in mind and body, but not particularly noted for gaiety or laughter. It might even be said that a person is a child of the environment in which he has his being, for the forces at work on his personality are so strong that he is either consciously or subconsciously molded in a pattern that fits the land in which he lives.

Any environment that produces the good things of life liberally and has a strong personality of its own is bound to produce its own life-style which will be a reflection of itself. So it is in the Napa Valley, which has evolved a way of life which is distinctly its own and is the envy of anyone who has ever sampled it. Given the beauty of this Valley, it is no wonder it exerts a charm so strong and pervasive that every year it claims thousands of willing victims.

Wine lands are traditionally happy lands, where laughter and song make up as much a part of the fabric of life as does hard work. When there is work to be done, it is done willingly, but laughter speeds the weary hours and helps lighten what would otherwise be an intolerable load. When the crush is done and the new wines are slumbering in their oaken cradles, then there is time for fun and relaxation, for gaiety and song to celebrate a task well done. The early wine festivals were always tied to the end of the harvest period; if they sometimes got a bit exuberant, it was only because the celebrants entered into the spirit of things and — like a new wine — sometimes got out of hand.

The Napa Valley is no exception to this general rule. In fact, it has developed a few traditions of its own, some of which have been handed down from the various sources of the Valley's culture, and others which have evolved from local conditions. Like all wine lands, it is a place where the local social customs are tied to the phases of the wine year, from the comparative quiet of summer to the frenetic activity of the crush.

Climate is always a major factor in determining the social customs of a region, and here the Valley is singularly blessed. Shielded by its mountains and inland location — yet adjacent to a major body of water — the climate is generally Mediterranean with a rainy yet mild winter and spring; a warm, sometimes hot summer; and an autumn that can drag seductive, summer-like days into early November. It is a climate made to order for outdoor living and entertainment, in which the Valley fully indulges. Outdoor entertaining is the order of the day, with most social functions during all but the three rainiest months taking place out-of-doors. The tremendous success of the Charles Krug August Moon programs and the Robert Mondavi Summer Series can be traced not only to the general excellence of the programs, but also to the beautiful surroundings in which they are held. There is something about relaxing on a well kept lawn in the shadow of the encircling mountains, and having one's senses lulled into a soothing euphoria by

Above: Lee Hodo relaxes around the pool on Saturday afternoon after spending the week handling public relations for Acacia Winery. Many homes in the Valley have their own pools, as outdoor swimming is possible almost year around. *Right:* The Mountain View Hotel pool in Calistoga is a very pleasant part of the good life in the Napa Valley.

good wine, good food, and good music that is extremely pleasant — an attainment of that good life which is the seldom achieved goal of people all over the world.

While the gentle climate and easygoing attitude of the Valley seemingly foster a casual state of life and attire, it is also a place that brings out the best in everyone. The natural sense of beauty that the Valley so freely evokes is evidenced — especially in the upper social levels — in beautiful accoutrements, clothes and manners. The style of living, by long association, seems perfectly natural to the inhabitants of the Valley, but is of a superlatively high order to others accustomed to a different level. Small wonder it is that the Napa Valley life-style has become the envy of those forced by fate to exist in other, less favored locales.

This way of life has the force of tradition, for from its very earliest days the Valley enjoyed an eclectic culture derived from the people who had elected to make this place their home. The Krugs, Schrams, de Latours, Carpys, Beringers, and Parrots were all well educated, cultured people with a natural sense of beauty and decorum. They early established codes of conduct and behavior that became the rules for the Valley. Those rules, set in a gentler, more formal era, have achieved the status of tradition over the years and are largely followed even to this day. They may be a little old fashioned — like the streetlights of St. Helena — but if so, they are delightfully old fashioned and usually very much appreciated, even by young people who have not been over-exposed to this type of living. The fact that these are the people who have the most enthusiasm for the Valley and its way of life would seem to indicate that the values exemplified here are basic and desirable to people of all ages and social strata.

The high degree of sophistication so evident in the Valley can be traced partly to this tradition of eclecticism, as well as to the fact that living costs here are so high that newcomers have usually had the cultural advantages affluence fosters. Many of the new vintners in the Valley are people who have attained considerable success in other fields of endeavor but have found in the wine scene a more desirable way of life — and in the Napa Valley a place where that way of life can be implemented. Thus, Fred McCrea came from the field of advertising, Jack Davies from business management, Mike Stone from the paper business, Donn Chappellet from automated food vending, and Joe Phelps from construction. These men brought not only the drive and expertise in business that had made them successes in their own fields, but also sophisticated living tastes that found a natural expression in the Valley. Others not directly connected with the wine scene also make the Valley their home. Arthur Hailey, for instance, when he isn't completely engrossed in writing his highly successful novels, splits his time between his home in the Bahamas and the Valley. The Valley abounds in talent of all kinds — often completely unrelated to the wine industry, but united in a common love for a place where life can be lived to the full, in the company of peple who are pleasant, productive, and compatible.

In a region that is largely rural and some distance from the amenities of a large urban center, it is only natural that hospitality in the home would take the place usually filled by nightclubs and fancy restaurants. And the hospitality of the Napa Valley is legendary! In a place where

Above: If this bottle could only talk! Part of the Joe Heitz collection which he acquired from the Crocker estate, it bears the date 1816 (the year after Waterloo!!) It was lovingly decanted at a dinner for ten convivial souls, along with a 1934 Chateau Latour, a 1929 Montrachet, a 1945 Beaulieu Cabernet Reserve, a 1964 Chateau Latour, a 1945 Mouton-Rothschild, and a hundred-year-old brandy that was a warm silken sunshine. This was truly an evening to remember — and part of the good life in the Napa Valley. *Right:* Not only does the aging room of Heitz Cellars hold priceless wines, it is also the scene of some very well appreciated dinners. Hospitality is legendary in the Napa Valley, and no one outdoes Joe and Alice Heitz.

seemingly every hostess has graduated from cooking school—or could have written the book—good cooking is taken for granted, and superlative cookery is common. The traditional fare of the world's wine countries has been supplemented here by the contributions of local cooks, some of whom have more than a touch of genius. When Simone Beck, the nationally renowned French Grande Dame of the gourmet world, put on a cooking school for a selected few students who wanted instructions in the very best — and were willing to put up $1,500 each to attend her course — it was only natural that she should hold her school in the Napa Valley. She drew passing marks from the Valley cooks who audited her course, but not the usual awe which was accorded her elsewhere.

As one who has feasted at the best tables in the Valley, I can testify that wine country cuisine is bountiful, inventive, and so tasty that a prolonged stay in the Valley poses a threat to the waistline that is overcome only with many hard sets of tennis. Good food goes naturally with good wine, and in the Italian style the two are inseparable. Since the life-style in the Valley is largely Italianate, it goes without saying that wine is part of every meal except breakfast and does much to foster the reputation of the Valley as a gastronomical paradise.

A flight over the Valley shows that swimming pools and tennis courts are an essential part of its way of life. Pools are in use nine months of the year, and tennis is a year-round sport. There are several well patronized golf courses in the Valley. One of them, the Silverado Country Club and Resort, is considered one of the best courses in the country and is often the site of very important tournaments. It includes a complex of tennis courts and swimming pools that makes it a very popular resort. Its condominiums also provide residences for people who believe that the charm of the Valley should be enjoyed on a year-round basis and who have the means to implement that belief. Horseback riding is a natural sport in these beautiful rolling hills, and the backroads are dotted with bike riders and backpackers enjoying a leisurely and closeup inspection of this, one of Nature's loveliest places. On any given day, the Valley is alive with joggers intent on working off excess pounds engendered by the region's good food, for the physical fitness craze is very strong in a Valley that prizes beauty in any form and is willing to work hard to attain it. Life is good in the Valley. Those who love it for the many facets of its attraction live the good life on a daily basis, taking it as a normal part of living in this delightful spot.

Life in the Valley is mostly rural, but that doesn't mean that it is deficient in cultural activities. St. Helena boasts the Silverado Museum, one of the finest small museums in the country. This is the gift of Norman Strouse, a retired advertising executive, who saw a chance to share with an appreciative public his collection of Robert Louis Stevenson memorabilia. Vintage Hall is another delightful museum, which is dedicated to the history of viticulture in the Valley from the earliest days to the present, an attraction that daily draws more and more people. The Napa Valley Symphony and Napa Community College are cultural assets of the first water, and the delightful nearby city of Napa has all the amenities of a small metropolis. For those who crave something more grandiose, San Francisco is only an hour away.

Above: Tuesday at 8:30 a.m. this group meets at JoAnn DePuy's court, perched on a high butte overlooking the Yountville Crossroad. After three hard sets, champagne served in silver goblets cools the fevered brow, making a pleasant match even better. *Right:* The Victorian Party, held at a beautiful old period mansion, not only benefits the Napa Valley Symphony, but also provides one of many pleasant social occasions that make life in the Valley so enjoyable.

One of the cultural assets of the Valley that is becoming increasingly popular and appreciated is the White Barn on Sulphur Springs Avenue in St. Helena. The labor of love of Nancy Garden, it is a turn-of-the-century carriage house whose loft has been renovated into a charming little theatre; the ground floor, complete with refurbished horse stalls, is used for community events and receptions. Long interested in the artistic life of the Valley, Nancy and her husband, David, have made available to the general public a charming little facility which does much to provide a place where the cultural talents of the Valley can find expression.

Some people live in the Valley and make their living in "The City," as San Francisco is universally designated. While the price and availability of gasoline may have some small effect on this arrangement, it will hardly destroy it. The people who can afford to commute to jobs in "The City" feel they have the best of two worlds, and they are not about to give up that delightful situation. High priced gasoline and rising at 5:00 A.M. are small prices to pay for the privilege of living in the Valley, especially when dawn breaking over the eastern mountain rim is such an entrancing spectacle.

God was indeed smiling the day He created the Napa Valley. Even if it did not produce some of the world's finest wines, it would still be a delightful spot in which to live. Enhanced as it is by Nature's gifts and the contributions of gifted men and women, it becomes the mecca of multitudes who feel that since they have but one life to live, they will live it in the most enchanting spot available. Unfortunately, it is not available to everyone, but still it can shine as a sought-after dream, a place of vicarious enjoyment that forever keeps alive the flame of hope and ambition.

As the poet Robert Browing put it, "Man's reach should exceed his grasp, or what's a Heaven for?"

Above: A wine tasting at Meadowood Resort Hotel, which benefits various enterprises at St. Helena High School, draws a large and appreciative crowd. *Right:* Part of Polly Solari's extensive collection of wine glasses from around the world, these glasses show the tastes of former centuries. Wine was not always as clear as it is today, and glasses were not only receptacles, but also, in their own right, art objects.

CHAPTER XIII

THE CHANGING VALLEY

Every year, the Valley claims thousands of new admirers who have gladly succumbed to her lush charms and the way of life exemplified here. Some of them even have the means to do something about it and become permanent residents. Once here, they usually become dedicated to keeping the Valley in an unchanged state so their Paradise may forever exemplify all the things that brought them here in the first place.

It is a forlorn hope, doomed to failure. The Valley is a living entity and, like all living things, subject to growth and change.

My first in-depth look at the Valley came in 1974 when I did the original research that led to this book. I willingly admit to having fallen head over heels in love with this beautiful place, and I have never deviated in my devotion to it. I must also admit that when I revisited my old love ten years later, there had been some changes. Like someone attending a high school reunion, one is often shocked to see the changes time has brought about.

Change is to be expected; nevertheless, it was a relief to find that some things had remained constant. The Valley still beautifully wears her seasonal robes of verdure, and changes them with grace and elegance; her hospitality is as effulgent as ever; and the wines, if it were possible, have become even better. Traffic is still a nightmare on Highway 29, but people will slow down with a smile to make room for you in the endless flow, and total strangers will greet you with a cheery "Good morning." St. Helena is still a throwback to a quieter, more sedate period in American life. The moon still caresses the Valley in a silvery, lambent light that is somehow different here from anywhere else in the world, with the possible exception of Tahiti. Some things are too good to change, and the beauty of the Napa Valley is one of them.

Still, there have been changes. A ride from Calistoga to Napa down the Silverado Trail furnishes a good example. At first the landscape seems unchanged; the Valley is still clothed in vineyards, with the craggy escarpments of the palisades to the east still towering over a region totally dedicated to viticulture. Cuvaison Winery, brand new in 1974, has become even more lovely with landscaping now come of age. It gracefully wears the general air of prosperity which is the rightful due of a winery that makes very good wine.

Then, a few miles down the road, the changes begin. First it is new residences and our first bed-and-breakfast house — a new phenomenon in the Valley, and one which has brought both benefits and problems. Then the roofs of Rombauer Vineyards peek from their forested knoll. This is a surprisingly large enterprise which not only produces its own excellent Chardonnay and Cabernet under its own label, but also provides services for many small wineries which have not yet established their own production facilities. The view of the Valley from the adjacent Rombauer residence, nestled among the trees on the forested hilltop, is one of the better ones in the Valley.

On the other side of the road, Chateau Boswell, with its twin turrets and stone facade, emulates a small

Above: A hot air balloon floats over a vineyard near Yountville—a never-to-be-forgotten experience that will probably get progressively better with the telling. *Right:* The old Parrot Estate on Spring Mountain Road is known to millions of television viewers as "Falcon Crest." Since 1974 it is also the everyday home of Mike and Susan Robbins.

chateau in the French wine country. It is one of several wineries along the Trail, some of which are so hidden by shrubbery and side roads that only the most determined seeker with a good map can find them.

Off Howell Mountain Road is the entrance to Meadowood Resort Hotel, which in just a few years has blossomed into the social heart of the Central Valley. A disastrous fire that totally destroyed the clubhouse in May 1984 only emphasized how engrained the resort had become in the Valley's social life. Needless to say, the clubhouse was rebuilt bigger and better than ever. With a fine golf course, six tennis courts that see almost constant usage, and an Olympic-sized swimming pool, it is a place where old friends meet, deals are made and acquaintances can ripen into new friendships. It was there in 1974, but not nearly as big, nor playing as large a part in the social life of the Valley. Unlike the much larger Silverado Country Club and Resort in Napa which primarily caters to a national clientele, Meadowood draws its clientele more from the Valley people. It is no coincidence that the Napa Valley Wine Auction is held here every year. To judge by the emphasis placed on things vinous, Meadowood's roots must be grape vines.

A bit farther down the Trail, Napa Creek Winery nestles among its oak trees. Seemingly a brand spanking new facility, it actually is one of the more mature buildings along the route, for this is the old Sunshine Meat Plant, expertly converted in 1980 to a winery. Owners Jack and Judy Schulze, made a real find here, for the sturdy old building had many of the features already built in that a modern winery needs, and in very short order they were producing five wines, among them some very well deserved award winners.

The next change is some miles down the Trail. Up a winding road to the left, the old Souverain Winery, renamed Rutherford Hill, has been greatly expanded with innovative rotary fermentators and a wine aging facility dug into the tufa of the eastern mountain slopes. The capacity of Rutherford Hill under owners Chuck Carpy and Bill Jaeger is in the process of being sharply expanded, since demand for their excellent Chardonnays, Cabernets, Pinot Noirs and Merlots has escalated to the point where it greatly exceeds supply. To provide the needed aging capacity, tunnels have been driven hundreds of yards into the mountainside. With two main tunnels and numerous laterals, the new facilities provide storage for over 6,500 barrels of wine.

Close by the winery is one of the more noticeable changes in the Valley. A new, very good restaurant — with prices to match — sits on the mountainside, commanding a magnificent view of the Valley. This is Auberge du Soleil, familiar to TV viewers of Falcon Crest as the place where many of the plots of the series are hatched, as lunch is served along with the intrigue. A condominium development is located nearby; its residents will never have to go very far for either an excellent lunch or a good bottle of wine.

Adjacent to the Rutherford Crossroad, the cream colored buildings of Conn Creek Winery contrast sharply with the green of adjacent vineyards. Owners Bill and Kathleen Collins built a beautiful home in 1978 in the Upper Valley where they have extensive vineyards. It was only natural that, being good business people, they should seek a higher return on their excellent grapes by converting them into wine, so Conn Creek Winery

Above: Inglenook Winery, steeped in the history of the Valley, has a fine wine library covering all periods of the winery's production. This is from the 1936 to 1964 period, one of Inglenook's finest. *Right:* The V. Sattui Winery and Cheese Shop is a friendly place to browse and shop on weekdays, while weekends find it bustling with customers.

came into existence. Since it is in the heart of the Cabernet and Chardonnay belts, these two wines are the mainstay of the winery although it has the capacity and expertise to produce most of the wines of the Valley.

As one proceeds southward on the Silverado Trail, the next new development to take the eye from the stunning vistas on every side is a picturesque pointed-arched set of buildings atop a knoll on the right. This is Silverado Vineyards, one of the newer and larger developments of recent years.

A call to the office is needed to open the decorative iron gates that bar the winding road to the winery. There the caller is treated not only to a beautiful view, but if the occasion demands, to some superlative wine. The winery has one distinction that sets it apart from any other winery in the Valley: there are no mousetraps in it, for this is a Disney Family enterprise, and in that organization Mickey is still something of a household pet.

This winery is indeed "state of the art." With a large and expanding capacity, it has not only the mandatory rows of steel fermentors and capacious barrel storage rooms filled with the best oak cooperage money can buy, but also the vineyards to complement the beautiful equipment. On a meticulously tended 180 acres adjacent to the winery, wine maker Jack Stuart is learning what those prime acres can produce, and from them he is making wine that does justice to those grapes. All the wines are excellent, but to me, the delicate Chardonnay is superb — a judgment borne out by numerous awards and medals already garnered by this comparatively new addition to the ranks of premium wineries in the Napa Valley. With a capacity of 50,000 cases a year, this is a winery to watch. Its future is predictably as bright as one of its white wines.

In the interest of continuity, it probably would be best to continue along the Silverado Trail, but as with any rule, there are bound to be exceptions to prove its validity. On the left side of the Trail, at number 6154, there is a private paved road that leads to a number of interesting additions to the Napa Valley scene. Let's take that road.

To the left, nestled in the foothills of Stag's Leap, are the buildings of Shafer Vineyards, an expression of the dreams of John and Bett Shafer. Like so many other recent additions to the Valley, John came from a completely different field — in his case, that of textbook publishing. On a knoll commanding a stunning view of the Middle and Lower Valley, they built what was to be their retirement home; but soon the Valley exerted her usual spell, and they began to dream of wine. They built their winery at the bottom of the hill. All thoughts of retirement have been shelved; they are much too busy making good wine and living the good life of the Napa Valley. As one who has tasted both the hospitality of this delightful couple and the wines they make, I can attest that Chicago's loss was the Napa Valley's gain.

If, instead of taking the left fork of the road, you took the right, you would enter a fold of the hills by way of a walnut bordered road that ends at a picturesque stone winery. When I first viewed it in 1974, it was in ruins, but it has been so expertly restored that today it looks as it did when it was first built in the 1890s. This is the home of Stags' Leap Vineyard, which, under the aegis of Carl Doumani, has emerged from its half-century of slumber, making one more winery fulfilling its destiny — that is, making fine wines. It has the usual comple-

Above: The plexiglass headed puncheons at Vichon Winery shows the sedimentation method that is characteristic of the wines produced here. It will be carefully filtered out before the wine is bottled. *Right:* Domaine Chandon is one of the largest facilities in the Napa Valley producing a sparkling wine. Never, in this French-oriented winery, is it referred to as "champagne."

ment of stainless steel fermentors and oak cooperage, and feeds from the vineyards at its doorstep.

The right side of the Trail houses another new development. Almost hidden from view, Pine Ridge looks like most other small wineries that have blossomed along the Trail. A closer look reveals that this is a 30,000-case facility, and capacity is being increased with a newly constructed addition. Wine maker Gary Andrus and his wife, Nancy, came from a ski-development background in Colorado in 1978 and established their winery on steep ground that requires terraced vineyards. The friendly, family-run facility is happily making wine and growing as demand dictates. Their Cabernets, Chenin Blancs and Chardonnays are the solid foundations on which their progress is built.

Continuing down the Trail and almost hidden on the left in its sheltering oaks, we find the buildings of Stag's Leap Wine Cellars. This winery has grown by leaps and bounds, especially since one of its Cabernets topped the lot in an international tasting — proving even to the chauvinistic French that the Napa Valley could not be dismissed from consideration, even by the eloquent Gallic shrug. To meet the demand, proprietor and wine maker Warren Winiarski has expanded his capacity but is still running behind, a situation he views with understandably mixed emotions. Neatly groomed and well staffed, this pretty little winery well deserves the high esteem in which it is held.

While Clos du Val, the next winery on the left, is not exactly a new development (since it made its first wine in 1972), it definitely is a facility which has attained maturity in the last decade. Owned by John Goelet, an American businessman, it is managed by Bernard Portet, whose father was for many years the wine maker at Chateau Lafite. Bernard's intent was, from the very first, to make Napa Valley wine — in the French manner. In this, he has succeeded very well; his Cabernets have been lauded as representing the best of Napa Valley qualities wedded to French finesse. Thoroughly American in his outlook and business methods, he is a Frenchman to the core when he approaches the dinner table — a fact amply brought out by the magnificent wines Clos du Val produces.

Clos du Val is not alone in this dedication to producing wine that is one of the accoutrements of good living. Another winery, at 3103 Silverado Trail, has raised this to the status of a fine art. Louis K. Mihaly is a transplanted Hungarian businessman who has carved out a very desirable niche for himself with his modern, state-of-the art winery. By choice, his is a comparatively restricted, discriminating clientele of fine restaurants and private clubs. His marketing building is often the scene of beautiful formal dinners, complete with candlelight, crystal, fine china and silverware — and of course, wine from an obvious source.

The vineyards now extend all the way to the Napa city limits and beyond. On Coombsville Road just outside the city, Bill Cadman has a small winery, Tulocay, where he lovingly makes a fantastic Pinot Noir. This routinely astounds people who think that this complex, temperamental wine can be made only in a large winery with unlimited technology available.

On the edge of San Pablo Bay, Acacia Winery, one of the southernmost in the Napa Valley, feeds from the vineyards of the Carneros region and proves conclusively that not all the best wine in the Valley is being made north of Yountville. There are several new wineries starting up as this part of the Valley begins to assert in wine what it has for many years proved in grapes.

Another recent development that undoubtedly will have a far reaching economic effect on this region is the establishment of the RMS (Remy Martin-Schramsberg) brandy distillery on Cuttings Wharf Road. A joint effort of the noted French brandy maker and the equally prestigious Schramsberg Vineyards, it has already brought a large ultra-modern plant to the Carneros region. This plant, paradoxically, uses century-old distillation techniques and provides a brand new market for those vintners who can produce wine suited to the making of fine brandy. With eight large copper alembic stills, hand crafted in the Cognac region of France, this plant vaguely looks like something transplanted from the eighteenth century, but a second, closer look will show the liberal use of computers and space age monitoring technology. It is a fascinating combination of the best methods modern science can produce wedded to the traditional ways that have withstood the test of time.

Heading up the Valley along Highway 29, there are more changes evident in new motels and bed-and-breakfast houses. Trefethen Vineyards on the right, long one of the premium vineyards in the Valley, is now transforming its grapes into wine in a newly constructed winery that blends so well with the older buildings that only an expert could tell which is the addition. On the left, Napa Wine Cellars, with its geodesic domed salesroom, does a brisk business selling its varietal wines; and farther up the road near the Oakville Grade, the expertly restored buildings of Far Niente loom out of surrounding groves of oaks. This was a ruin when I first viewed it in 1974, but today it has been transformed with attractive landscaping. The old stone building has been refurbished from top to bottom and is now busily fulfilling its destiny; it was built to make wine and that is what it is doing — and doing it extremely well.

Its neighbor on the Oakville Grade, Vichon Winery, can claim a different distinction. It was built on a site which was no one's first choice because of the difficulties of construction, but which turned out so well that now everyone is trying to take credit for it. Built into the side of a steep hill, it commands a magnificent view of the Middle Valley. This winery incorporates many French ideas in its wine making, including leaving the wine on the yeast for extended periods of time and aging its white wines in oaken puncheons. A very modern winery with a capacity of 50,000 cases, it is staffed with people who have all previously worked in other wineries and whose cumulative knowledge has been pooled to produce unusual and very superior wines. This winery has recently been acquired by Robert Mondavi.

Proceeding up the Valley, we come to Cakebread Cellars on the right, housed in two redwood buildings and producing award winning wines. Wine maker Bruce Cakebread is evidently a man who likes good wine; since he primarily drinks his own, he makes it very well. An especial treat at this winery was tasting the very scarce "Rutherford Gold," a silky smooth sweet botrytis wine that was a foretaste of Paradise.

One vintner who has shrewdly capitalized on the natural affinity between good food and wine is Daryl Sattui whose winery on Highway 29 in St. Helena is one of the busiest spots on a frenectically busy highway. Scion of an old wine making family, he early decided to become a vintner and to that effect toured Europe as a young man, picking up background knowledge. Returning to the United States long on knowledge but short on funds, he finally decided that the Napa Valley would be his home.

His is one of the genuine rags-to-riches stories in the Napa Valley rivaled only by that of Hanns Kornell. Scraping together $5,000.00, he took a lease on the present location of V. Sattui Winery and bought enough wine from other vintners to generate a cash flow. Trading on his European background, he also installed a small cheese and salami department in his tasting room.

The first few months were really a threadbare, hand-to-mouth experience with wine stored in his bedroom, more often than not a sleeping bag on the sales room floor. Little by little the fledgling operation began to turn a profit, which was immediately ploughed back into more stock to generate a greater income.

Right from the beginning, Daryl slanted his operation toward the European idea of consuming wine along with food — hence the picnic grounds in front of his sales room. Today they are so crowded that he sells his whole output of 16,000 cases yearly from this one outlet. The delicatessen brings in as much as the winery, and that is definitely considerable.

St. Helena hasn't changed that much. There are a few more bed-and-breakfast houses, but the town still has the charm that makes it one of the most delightful little towns in the country. The avenue of elms in front of the Beringer Vineyards is still putting up a valiant fight for survival, and the large complex of fermenting tanks on the right has somehow put on a patina of age that rescues it from the rawness that always seems to curse a new installation.

At the extreme end of Madrona Street the road rises in serpentine curves to culminate at the spectacularly located winery of Newton Vineyard. Enjoying a superb view of St. Helena and the Valley, it is notable for many things, but chiefly because its delightfully fresh wines are grown on terraces hacked out laboriously from the steep mountain terrain. Admittedly an expensive process, owners Peter and Su Wah Newton felt the expense was justified because their aim was to make the best wine their vineyards could possibly produce. Anyone tasting the crisp, clean whites or elegant full-bodied reds must agree that those old timers who preferred mountain grown grapes knew a thing or two about wine.

For many years one of the most photographed houses in St. Helena has been the gabled Victorian home set on a hillside to the left of the highway. Directly behind the house but hidden from the road, there is a little gem of a stone winery that is one of the best kept secrets in the Napa Valley. It looks as though it has been there for decades, but actually it is of recent construction — the brainchild of Dr. William Casey, an ophthalmologist turned wine maker. A masterpiece of attention to detail, it is no wonder that the Chardonnays, Sauvignon Blancs and Cabernets issuing from it under the St. Clement label are so good; they reflect the same care that went into the building of the winery.

There are other evidences of change as one proceeds up the Valley. The old cement works has been converted into a complex of shops and restaurants; the Bale Mill has become a state park; and off to the right down a long lane, Charles Shaw has built his residence and winery. Here, using the "maceration carbonique" method used in the Beaujolais region of France, he converts Gamay grapes into a sprightly young wine that is usually on the market by November 15 of the year in which it was vinted. He makes the practically obligatory Cabernet also, but his Gamay Nouveau and some shrewd marketing have been a large part of his success.

And so it goes, all over the Valley. It would be impractical to list all the new wineries — even if it were possible — for the Valley is in a state of flux. Every year those who predict that the Valley has finally reached her greatest possible development are confounded. Some of the new wineries, such as Raymond Vineyard and Cellar on Zinfandel Lane, are large enterprises making excellent wine, while others are comparatively small, proving you do not have to be big to be good. Some specialize, like Silver Oak Cellars which makes only Cabernets, or Peju Province which makes a specialty of its Sauvignon Blanc. Others diversify, making whatever wine the best grapes they can buy will produce.

New enterprises come from all over, many of them founded by affluent people who are enamoured of the Valley life-style and see in the acquisition of a winery a quick entry into what they believe is a charmed circle. Some, however, are deeply rooted in the Valley. Raymond Vineyard and Cellar, for instance, is owned and operated by a family famous in the Valley, with ties to the pioneer Beringer brothers. Their modern, 50,000-case winery can produce anything well, but to me, their Chardonnay has a special charm, even in a Valley teeming with good Chardonnays.

One of the better changes in the Napa Valley over the last decade or so has been the proliferation of restaurants that exploit the natural marriage of good food and fine wines. It used to be that the fare in the few available restaurants, with one or two notable exceptions, ran to tough, overdone steaks and vulcanized chicken — with little or no choice left for the person with a discriminating palate. This situation was all the more deplorable because the fare in the private homes ran from excellent to superb. People accustomed to superior food at home were not about to have their palates insulted by an evening out. Then a good restaurant or two, with fare reflecting the good cookery that is the natural legacy of wine lands came into the Valley and prospered mightily. Within a year the rush was on.

Today the Valley from Calistoga to Napa is dotted with excellent restaurants, featuring imaginative menus and fine wine lists, that reflect the bounty available at their doorsteps. One can eat the finest French cooking, authentic Italian or hearty German fare the length of the Valley, with choice governed only by the depth of one's appetite or pocketbook. Spectacularly situated restaurants such as the Auberge du Soleil offer not only an elevated view of the Valley, but also a high level of culinary artistry, with prices to match. More moderately priced restaurants are available, but often are tucked away on side streets and known only to the locals or the gastronomic cognoscenti. These people rate the finding of a good, relatively inexpensive restaurant as a pearl of great price and usually try to keep the place a secret so it will not be ruined by popularity.

The fame of the Valley as a place where the natural beauty of the surroundings is complemented by good food and wine is spreading rapidly — so much so that a growing number of people from the metropolitan area of San Francisco think nothing of making the sixty-mile trek to the Valley for lunch or a leisurely paced dinner. And practically always, along with the fine food, the superb wines of the Napa Wine Country are sipped appreciatively, adding that special touch that makes a good meal memorable.

Another change in the Valley has been in overnight housing. Ten years ago the Valley was a place where you spent a very pleasant day or evening but went elsewhere to spend the night. Lodging in the Valley, with a few exceptions, ran from inadequate to downright non-existent. That is changing, although at certain times of year and in some parts of the Valley there can be more people wanting to spend the night than there are beds to accommodate them. To fill this demand, the hotel industry has been expanding capacity in the Valley and a few people with large homes began offering rooms for the night with breakfast served in the morning. It didn't take long for the bed-and-breakfast idea to catch on — and with a vengeance!

Ever alert to any change that might damage the Valley's fragile charm, the powers that be saw to it that laws were passed limiting the number of rooms that could be rented to three per household. The laws were sometimes circumvented, or in a few ignoble cases, brazenly ignored. Someone with a large home, a good view, an adequate swimming pool and an aggressive lawyer just might feel that the potential income would generate a large bank balance ... and therefore feel justified in skirting the law. This problem is one of the growing pains that face the Valley, making many people wish that the old days, when the Valley was for day visitors only, would return. They might as well stop wishing; time does not turn backward.

There are some handsome new hostelries that have been legitimately established in the Valley and more are planned which will provide greater lodging choices. The Valley is an "in" place and, like anything that is desirable and in limited quantity, is apt to be expensive.

Another facet of the Valley today does not constitute so much a change as it does an acceleration of a trend that was already well under way a decade ago. Ever since the Valley was first settled by white men, its beauty has attracted international attention. Many people willingly succumbed to the spell the Valley casts so effortlessly and decided to make it their permanent home. Laws designed to keep the Valley largely as an agricultural preserve inhibit the development that would long ago have swallowed up the whole Valley in asphalt paving. Therefore, the choice spots that are available are highly priced. As a result, many of the newcomers to the Valley are people with substantial resources. The attraction of the Valley is not only the natural beauty of the region, but also the life-style that has evolved here, and most of the new arrivals gladly immerse themselves in it. Inevitably, however, some vestiges of their former life-styles remain and are often incorporated into the new way of life they have adopted in the Valley.

While it must be admitted that most of the new arrivals gladly adopt the endemic life-style of the Valley, there are enough affluent, hedonistically inclined exceptions to give the new Valley a definitely different touch. For that reason, people who are not directly involved in

Above: The copper alembic stills at R. M. S. Distillery were crafted in Cognac, France, in a style that has stood the test of centuries. *Right:* Bernard Skoda has good reason to smile; his vineyards and winery in Rutherford are some of the best in the Valley.

the wine scene are somehow apart from the mainstream of Valley life. These have a tendency to cluster together in a somewhat separate society where they feel more at home discussing golf and high finance, and drinking martinis rather than wine. A gradual melding of the two styles is inevitable, but it is also undeniable that the new arrivals are coloring the social life and economy of the Napa Valley.

Because the Valley is so dominated by the wine scene, it is often forgotten that there are other underpinnings to its prosperity; indeed, it was not till 1972 that wine outdistanced stock-raising as the largest industry in the Valley. There are still large ranches in Napa County, but they are mostly concentrated in the surrounding mountains. The flatland and gentle slopes have long since been usurped by vineyards. Stock-raising is still very important, but so dominated by wine that not one person in ten ever thinks of it when the Napa Valley is mentioned. Tourism and the ancillary services associated with it are a never ending treasure lode, but the underlying fact is that Napa Valley is synonymous with fine, and even superb, wine.

This fact is generally well known to most Californians, or anyone at all familiar with good wine; letting the rest of the world know it is another matter. That the Napa Valley apellation is indeed synonymous with fine and usually superlative wine is about as accurate as any generalization can get. It is well known in the Valley that if a winery survives for five years, it is doing one of two things: it is either making very good wine or it is digging into some very deep pockets. While deep pockets are not exactly unknown in the Valley, good wine is much more common and is the general rule. For that reason, the appellation "Napa Valley" is generally regarded as a cachet of vinous nobility. Even the uninitiated wine drinker can be secure in the knowledge that any bottle bearing this label has a better-than-even chance of being very good, or even superb.

At the forefront of this effort is the Napa Valley Vintners' Association, with membership open to those who have an established winery and have demonstrated fiscal responsibility. This organization has the social and business betterment of its members and the industry as a whole as its prime reason for existence; it is also the spearhead for any movement that will benefit the Valley and the people living in it. It is a central point where useful information can be exchanged, or where concerted action can originate if the need for it arises.

A good example of how concerted action can help the whole Valley is the Napa Valley Wine Auction, which in the space of a few years has become one of the most prestigious in the whole world. Started with the idea of benefitting the Valley's hospital facilities, it quickly grew into something much bigger—a first-class media event, with well-heeled collectors converging on Meadowood from all over the world. The hospitals have undoubtedly benefitted from the auction of donated wines, but the Valley has also reaped a harvest of the finest publicity possible. It also is a first-class party—as anyone who has had the fortune of attending it will attest — but then, that is expected. The Napa Valley is definitely a first-class act, and anything pertaining to it is expected to shine with the same lustre.

The Valley is so well suited to the growth of world class Chardonnays and Cabernets that it undoubtedly

Above: Alf Burtleson is known locally as "The Cave Man," since he has excavated numerous caverns in the Valley which serve as energy efficient wine aging facilities. *Right:* These temperature-controlled stainless steel fermentation tanks at Silverado Vineyards are "state of the art."

will continue in that role, but some changes are already apparent in the popularity of other wines. Many mature vineyards planted to Zinfandel are being replanted in other grapes, as this once popular grape gradually is being displaced by other varieties. Zinfandel has been considered the most Californian of all red wines for many years, but recently its partisans have been split into so many factions that no group can command the following that makes the production of any one type of wine economically feasible. White Zinfandel seems to be the exception to this rule, with over one hundred wineries producing it in 1984, but it is of definite significance that practically all of these wineries are outside the Napa Valley.

The same can be said of Johannisberg Riesling, once one of the most popular wines produced in the Valley. The problem seems to be land that will grow good Riesling will usually also grow Chardonnay, and the latter brings a better price. Specialists like Bernard Skoda of Rutherford Vintners will probably always make Johannisberg Riesling and find a ready market for it, but he does so largely because he has a devoted cadre of followers who, by preference, value that wine above all others.

If any grape can be said to be the grape of the future, it probably would be Merlot. Long grown in the Gironde region of France as a blending grape for the famous Cabernets of Bordeaux, it was brought to California for the same purpose. The soil in which it is grown, as well as the climate, have much to do with the final characteristics of any grape; in California, Cabernet Sauvignon developed qualities quite different from those achieved in its native France. It was much softer than the often acerbic grapes of Bordeaux and not nearly as dependent on the ameliorating effects of Merlot.

The same qualities of soil and climate that wrought changes in Cabernet also made changes in Merlot, and it was not long before it was noticed that this soft, blending wine achieved a nobility which, with one notable exception, it had never quite reached in France. It was experimentally bottled as a varietal; but every year, growing numbers of enthusiastic devotees of this soft, yet full bodied wine demand that it be produced in quantity. If the number of vineyards now being replanted to Merlot are any indication (and most observers believe they are), in the 1990s Merlot may very well usurp the place formerly held by Zinfandel.

Another change in the Valley is quite recent but is also an echo of something that was in vogue a hundred years ago. Back in the days before commercial refrigeration was readily available, the cool temperature necessary for the fermentation and storage of fine wines was achieved by using caves dug into the mountainsides. With the advent of modern refrigeration, the caves were relegated to the status of tourist attractions, colorful anachronisms, although wineries that had usable tunnels continued to use them for storage. Then it was noticed that caves had a practically unlimited lifespan, and that their energy requirements and upkeep were minimal. Modern methods of excavation, compared to the pick-and-shovel methods used by the Chinese coolies who first dug the tunnels of the Napa Valley, brought the cost down to the point that the caves once more became an economic feasibility. In a short time the rush was on.

Alf Burtleson is a very enterprising contractor who figured that coal mining techniques could be adapted to

Above: Using coal-mining techniques, a workman excavates a cavern for Rutherford Hill Winery, while another hauls out the detritus. *Right:* Flora Springs Winery, nestled at the western edge of the mountain wall, is a former ghost winery. It has now been completely renovated as a family enterprise and is busily making excellent Cabernet, Chardonnay, and Sauvignon Blanc.

the sandstone and volcanic ash soils of the Napa Valley hillsides. His judgment has been vindicated. Already, he has dug extensive caves in the Sonoma Valley, and the large caverns he has excavated for Anderson Vineyards, Schramsberg, and Rutherford Hill have earned him the soubriquet of "The Cave Man." He should have no worry about running out of projects, as the comparatively large outlay needed to dig a cave is offset in the long run by the lower maintenance costs and general efficiency of this type of installation. Anyone with a hillside close to his winery is either planning to dig into it, or is at least giving it some serious thought.

For those who don't have suitable terrain for a cavern and cannot quite justify the horrendous costs of building an above-ground aging facility, there is another alternative: the cooperative warehouse where aging space can be leased. This is an attractive idea, borne out by the fact that one such large facility in St. Helena never seems to be completed; as fast as an addition is finished, it is fully leased and a new addition is started. To a small or even a medium sized winery faced with mushrooming growth due to demand, this can be a lifesaver.

Almost any morning when the winds are not gusting and it is not raining, hot air balloons ride gracefully over the Valley. This, too, is an escalation of a trend that already was well under way in 1974. In those days it was common to see two or three balloons lazily drifting over the vineyards, the sibilant blasts of their burners the only sound breaking the silence. Today, it is not uncommon to see a dozen or so aloft at the same time and it is a rare moment when you cannot hear a balloon.

Yountville, because of its central position in the Valley, has become the center of ballooning activities; at least one firm actively engaged in providing a balloon's-eye view of the Valley — Adventures Aloft — makes its headquarters there. Depending on which way the breezes are blowing, the happy passengers are wafted aloft to cruise over the vineyards of the Upper or Lower Valley, sometimes low enough to literally pluck a cluster of grapes from the rows just beneath the gondola. Such a ride is guaranteed to be the main topic of conversation long after other aspects of the Valley have faded into a euphoric haze. A chase car follows on the network of back roads that crisscross the Valley, so grounding crews are always close at hand when the flight is finally brought to ground.

There have been so many new wineries established in the Valley that trying to list all of them would be futile. Besides, any published list would be outdated ten days after it was published. I do, however, apologize to all those winery owners whom I have not mentioned in this chapter. It certainly was not deliberate, but rather an expression of the growth that has taken place in the Valley. The days when the Valley could easily be visited in a day or two are long gone; today, it would take weeks or even months to visit all the wineries that are in operation in the confines of what was once a small valley. I spent almost three months there, actively seeking out new wineries — and I didn't get to see all of them. Suffice it to say, I look upon these wineries as a backlog of delightful places still to be discovered, of new wine makers still to be met, of new wines still to be tasted; for my love of this Valley is not a passing fancy, but a very real, vital part of my life and one which I intend to indulge as long as I am able.

ৰ

Above: A glass of good Napa Valley wine, an apple, a piece of cheese, and some good crisp French bread make a recipe for complete enjoyment. *Right:* The lifestyle in the Napa Valley is exemplified by Dana and Hilary DePuy. The setting is also used as Richard Channing's home in "Falcon Crest."

CHAPTER XIV

OF VINES AND MEN

Critics of American wines have a few favorite subjects that they belabor unceasingly. While some of these criticisms are merely personal judgments that are expounded at length because a large part of the pleasure attendant to wine drinking comes from talking about it, others have a solid basis in fact and are worthy of discussion on their own merit. Of these, one of the most often discussed is the matter of names for wine.

Back in the early days of the wine industry, when the clientele was not nearly so sophisticated, names didn't matter much. Wine was bought by the barrel, was either white or red, and as long as it was potable, was accepted at face value without too much worry as to its pedigree. As quantity and quality increased and wine became a major item of commerce, individual vintners sought to identify their product by a recognizable name, so the need arose to identify the wine more fully.

Count Agoston Haraszthy inadvertently solved one problem—and created another—when he brought back from Europe thousands of grape cuttings that were to provide the vines for the California wine industry. With a few notable exceptions, these cuttings were identified by species and places of origin. This provided an easy, if not wholly accurate, way to identify the wines soon to be made from the grapes sprouting from those cuttings.

A number of facts soon became apparent from the Haraszthy project; one of the most startling was that wine made from grapes grown in California could be, and usually was, far different from that made from that same species in its native land. A Cabernet grown in California had a fullness and softness quite unlike that grown in Bordeaux, a fact that often made 100% varietal wines a possibility. Vintners have long known that climate and soil induce changes in the vine and the fruit it bears; here, in this new land with its rich, undepleted soil, a completely different kind of grape was being grown. It is true that the main characteristics of the parent vine were retained, but the differences were great enough to be discernible even to the untrained palate.

Purists argued that any change from the classic grapes of Europe were deficiencies, but more pragmatic persons who had tasted the new wines were quick to note that the differences were not necessarily bad, and in some cases were very definite improvements.

It must be remembered that the infant wine industry in California was still tied by tradition to the established wine countries of Europe. Also the newly affluent American public tended to look down on any wine produced in America as definitely inferior. Since these constituted a good part of the new industry's potential clientele, their wishes, of necessity, were considered. So the magnificent new wines of the Napa Valley were marketed under names like "California Burgundy" or "Chablis," which they definitely were not.

Immediately after Prohibition the opportunity to give meaningful names to the wine produced in the Valley was once more presented, and again rejected in the name of expediency. So to this day, we have a generic name like "Burgundy" covering anything made with red grapes, and "Chablis" referring to practically any still white wine that is not rosé or sherry.

Above: A man in his element, Peter Mondavi is at home in his vineyard with a glass of his own good wine in his hand. *Right:* It is summer's end, and this cluster of Pinot Noir grapes, dusty and slightly sunburned, is ready for picking.

In spite of the fact that the wine snob has a tendency to look down on the generic wines, they are usually good, honest wines, and often very fine value. I know of one "Burgundy" which I bought in quantity in 1976, for I was there in 1974 when a load of prime Cabernet Sauvignon grapes unexpectedly filled the Cabernet tank to capacity before half the load was crushed. The balance, for lack of fermenting space, went into the "Burgundy" tank, much to the vintner's chagrin. He had to pay Cabernet prices for a wine which was largely from a noble grape, but which he had to sell at a much lower price. His loss was the customer's gain, for that wine in spite of its humble name had most of the characteristics of the much higher priced Cabernet Sauvignon.

With the growing importance and reputation of Napa Valley, attention is once more being given to the idea of naming wines produced in the Valley with the names that have some local connection. "Rutherford" may not sound as elegant as "Chateau Latour," but the wine produced there can be equally good; the public would soon learn the names they equate with quality. Also under consideration is the idea of a bottle with a distinctive shape that would say "Napa" as eloquently as the bottles of Bordeaux or Burgundy identify their own regions. There are some good brains working on this idea whose possessors are not in the habit of wasting their time.

There was much talk around 1975, especially by wine writers who did their writing without doing fieldwork, of the overproduction of wine grapes that supposedly would peak in 1977. It was true there had been many new plantings that would start producing about that time and the then-existing facilities would be unable to accommodate them, but even in a region as predictably productive as the Napa Valley, there can be changes in the usual pattern. The years 1976 and 1977 were just such years.

Two circumstances intervened to prevent a monstrous grape glut in Napa Valley. First was a two-year drought that drastically cut yields, so instead of a glut, there actually was a shortage. Then, too, there was at the same time an explosion of publicity about the Valley. New people with ample money to spend poured into the Valley and with unprecedented speed built new facilities that almost doubled the Valley's capacity to produce fine wines. Today, practically all the land in the Valley suited to viticulture is planted in fine varietals, and the Valley boasts over a hundred bonded wineries, ready, able and eager to convert those grapes into superb wines. New wineries seeking their own vineyards are either hacking them out of the mountainsides at prohibitive prices or paying equally prohibitive prices to vineyardists who are ready to retire and, with this sale, can now do so in the grand manner.

The new emphasis in the Napa Valley is toward varietal wines, partly because they can command a better price, but also because these wines best exploit the characteristics of the Valley's soil and climate. The Valley seemingly can grow anything in the vinifera family—and very well. In 1973 and again in 1977, it even proved that a hitherto unattained goal was possible.

Freemark Abbey is very fortunate that three of its general partners own extensive and excellent vineyards in the Valley. Naturally, these men see to it that their best grapes find a home in their own winery. In September 1973 there were two days of drizzly rain, followed by warm and humid weather, conditions much desired in

Above: Family roots run deep in the Napa Valley where wine making goes on from generation to generation. Here a busy, active mother still has time to love and be loved by her children. *Right:* A concert at the White Barn in St. Helena usually features very good local talent and equally good local wines.

212

the Sauternes region of France, because it fosters the growth of *botrytis cinerea,* the "noble rot" that produces the sweet and luscious wines for which the region is famous. Laurie Wood noticed that a large section of his Conn Creek vineyard was infested with a mold that had all the classic appearance of botrytis. Tests proved that it was indeed the much-sought-after "noble rot," and thirty-six tons of grapes were affected by it.

Botrytis penetrates the skin of a grape and draws off the moisture, thus increasing the sugar content. Those White Riesling grapes at harvest had a sugar content of 30° B and produced a heavy, sweet wine very much like the wines of Sauternes and quite unlike the usual Johannisberg Riesling they normally would have made. The wine is a classic—worth whatever price the vintner puts on it—because those conditions that produced it are a "once-in-a-lifetime" proposition that may never again be repeated, much as one might desire it.

The slogan, "cities are what people make them," is well known and can be applied as well to the Napa Valley; not only does the Valley mold the character of the people who make this their home, but it has itself been shaped by the men and women who have lived in this place. Charles Krug, Gustave Niebaum, the Beringer brothers, Charles Carpy, Georges de Latour, Jacob Schram, and more lately John Daniel and Louis Martini — all have left their mark on this Valley and have influenced the lives of the men who today carry on the work they started.

The pioneer wine makers would be proud of the new breed that carry on the tradition of excellence that they founded. Andre Tchelistcheff, the legendary wine maker of Beaulieu Vineyards, is retired now but is still active as a consultant, and the men he trained are leaders in the industry. One doesn't become a leader in this industry without having some very positive ideas about wine, and it is not at all unusual to find diametrically opposite views on the same subject emanating from people who each have a cadre of devoted followers. The wonderful thing about this situation is that these people can differ strongly on some facet of wine making, yet be close personal friends and mutual admirers. There are, however, a few people who seemingly rise above all others and are held in high esteem by all. Two of these certainly would be Brother Timothy of The Christian Brothers and Hanns Kornell.

Brother Timothy's long period of service in the Napa Valley alone would entitle him to respect, but it is the man's basic kindness that most endears him to his friends. A shrewd bargainer and a hard competitor, he nevertheless would be the first to extend a helping hand to anyone needing it; it is this fact that most endears him to his peers.

Hanns Kornell is a unique combination of generosity, honesty, and integrity blended with a generous dosage of talent. An immigrant from Germany, he has become such an integral part of the Valley that it seems he must have been born here. There is no other Hanns Kornell in Germany (or for that matter anywhere else in the world), but if there were, the air fare to the Napa Valley could easily be raised by popular subscription; such is the popularity of the genial German from Mainz.

A list of the interesting or productive people in the Valley would simply be a roster of the vintners doing business there. It is a place that fosters quality, and the

Above: Hanns Kornell is certainly one of the most popular and respected citizens in the Napa Valley today. However, he likes to recall that back in 1940, as a practically penniless refugee from Nazi Germany, he spent a night in the Calistoga jail because he wasn't carrying the proper papers. A plaque saying "Hanns Kornell slept here" wouldn't seem out of place now. *Right:* What an elegant setting for an aristocrat of wine! The 1973 Freemark Abbey Edelwein is a once-in-a-lifetime experience that demands, and gets, the very finest care. *Overleaf:* Spring is a time for awakening, and the almond trees etch a pattern of lacy white blossoms against a blue sky near the Carmelite Monastery, looking toward the eastern mountains.

track is so fast that only the best survive. Men like Joe Heitz, Chuck Carpy, Robert and Peter Mondavi, Louis Martini, Joe Phelps, Jack Davies, Brother Timothy, Daryl Sattui and Donn Chappellet, to name only a few, can't help but make a place electric with their own personal magnetism; even a few minutes spent with these men shows why they have achieved success and risen to the top of their profession. It takes talent, hard work, and drive to be a vintner anywhere, but in the Napa Valley, where the race is held between the admitted leaders in the field, these qualities are the bare minimum. It's that little extra touch of genius that makes the difference; when that quality was being handed around, the Valley's vintners went around for a second helping.

What does the future hold for the Valley? That, of course, is unknown, although some reasonably safe predictions based on available data can be made.

As America becomes more conscious of things vinous and more appreciative of the wines produced here, the Napa Valley can expect to increase its already dominant share of the market for fine table wines. More and more people are discovering that fine wine is one of the more worthwhile pleasures in life and are taking part in that experience by laying down stores of choice vintages in their own cellars, so wines acquired in their youth can mature into the nobility which is their natural heritage. While a Napa Valley Cabernet may be completely drinkable at four years of age, it will improve immeasurably if it is laid away to bottle age and achieve the silky smoothness and character that only time can give. Drinking such a wine when it is young is an act of infanticide, but it inevitably will be done until Americans learn that the fruits of patience can be very rewarding—and act accordingly. Fortunately, the trend is growing. Good cellars are proliferating; in them, the noble wines of the Napa Valley sleep, patiently waiting for the time when their bounty will be released and add a touch of beauty to the life of man.

As for the Valley itself, it will almost certainly continue to be a rural area, unless complete madness engulfs the powers that decide these things. It will certainly continue its dedication to quality, because that fits with the Valley's character and has proven that it is the right path to take. As America becomes more sophisticated in things vinous, the Valley certainly will be more appreciated and come into its own. The people there hopefully will retain the way of life they have evolved and guard it zealously, so their children may someday enjoy an enclave of beauty in an increasingly developed world.

It is that beauty that haunts people who have been exposed to it, for the need for beauty is as deep and basic, as deeply rooted in the soul of a sensitive person, as is the need for food and drink. It is no wonder my memory often wanders back to the Valley, seeing again the delicate tracery of light and shadow on the face of Mt. St. Helena and roaming once more those verdant hills, blue with the lupine of spring or tawny with the gold of summer. I see the vineyards blossom yellow with mustard, grow green with summer, and wear once more their autumnal robes of purple and gold. I see the fruit hang on the vine, swollen with nectar, inviting one to taste its sweetness, and I know that once more, in spirit, I am in my beloved Napa Valley...

I lift my glass to you.

Above: White blossoms against an azure sky, the humming of bees, the caress of a gentle breeze — this is spring in the Napa Valley. *Right:* It is easy to tell red wine grapes from white once the colors of autumn have painted the vines. Red grape leaves turn red in the foreground and distance; white grape leaves turn gold in the middle of this vineyard along the eastern mountain rim near Stag's Leap.

GLOSSARY

Aging: The process wherein wine is stored in oaken barrels or casks, so complex changes that only time implements can take place in the wine. Aging smooths a rough, new wine, adds bouquet and character. Most aging takes place in an oaken tank or barrel, although some changes also take place in the bottle.

Alluvial fans: Soil deposits brought down from the mountains by streams and deposited in the Valley.

Aroma: The particular odor of a specific grape. Not to be confused with bouquet, although a wine has both.

Basket press: A type of press wherein grapes are put in a wooden tub with slotted sides. Pressure applied by means of a large screw crushes the grapes and allows the juice to run out through the slots. Used only in small wineries.

Big wine: A wine of powerful and distinctive characteristics.

Botrytis cinerea: A fungus which dries up the moisture in a grape and raises sugar content. Very desirable, in spite of its unprepossessing appearance.

Bouquet: The special scent a wine gives off after it is poured. Bouquet results from aging, both in the tank and in the bottle.

Burger: A white wine grape, formerly very popular in the Valley as the basis for Chablis. Now not very popular and rapidly being replaced.

Cap: The mass of grape skins, pulp, and seeds that floats over the fermenting grape juice. (Red wine only.)

Cabernet Franc: A red wine grape, popular in France as a blending agent. Not generally grown in the Valley.

Cabernet Sauvignon: A red wine grape, originally the great grape of the Bordeaux region. Although a sparse bearer it is popularly conceded to yield the greatest red wine of the Napa Valley.

Cellarman: A worker in a winery who transfers wine, scrubs fermenting tanks, etc.

Centrifuge: A machine which uses the principle of centrifugal force to clear particulate matter from wine. Although power driven, it operates on the same principle as the old cream separator.

Chablis: A generic name for wine made from almost any white grape. Named after the Chablis Region in France.

Champagne: In the United States, just about any naturally fermented sparkling wine. In France, only those sparkling wines that originate in the district of Champagne. Thus, American champagne wines, even very good ones, may not be sold in France as "champagne."

Charmat process: A method of making champagne whereby the wine is fermented in a large container and bottled under pressure without fermentation taking place in the bottle.

Chardonnay: Also sometimes called Pinot Chardonnay. A noble white grape originally from Burgundy, from which a big, full white wine is made.

Coastal Zone: One of the five climatic zones into which grape growing areas are divided. The Coastal Zone is of medium warmth.

Continuous press: A wine press in which the grape pulp is fed in and the press wine and pomace extracted continuously.

Crush: The time of year during which the grapes are harvested and turned into wine, usually late August to early November in the Valley.

Crushing: The process whereby the grapes are broken open and juice is liberated.

Degrees Balling: A scale method of measuring sugar content in grape juice. Usually marked ° B. It is also known as Brix.

Estate bottling: Designation given a wine which is totally produced on the winery's property. All the grapes are grown in the winery's vineyards, and all the operations from crushing to bottling are performed in the winery's cellars.

Falling bright: A spontaneous clearing of suspended material from wine without outside help.

Fermentor: Any container used to ferment grape juice into wine. Formerly made of wood or concrete, they are now made mostly of glass or stainless steel.

Fining: The process of clearing the wine of any suspended material.

Flora: A hybrid grape which was developed at the University of California at Davis. It has a sweet taste similar to the Traminer.

Free run: The juice that results from the first crushing of the grapes, without pressing.

French Colombard: An aromatic white wine grape, or the wine made from it. Almost always used as a blending grape in France, it is increasingly popular in the Napa Valley as a varietal.

Gamay: A red wine grape, originally from the Beaujolais Region in France, now grown extensively in the Napa Valley. It produces a fruity, light red wine, best drunk when young.

Generic (wines): A wine named after the region in which it originated, or which has the general characteristics of such a wine.

Golden Chasselas: A heavy-bearing white wine grape once very popular in the Valley, but now being largely replaced. Also called "Palomino."

Gondola: A wheeled open-topped horizontal tank that is used to collect grapes.

Green Hungarian: A white wine grape, often made into a varietal in the Napa Valley. Origin unknown, in spite of the name.

Jug wine: Wine of no particular breed or standing, which is usually sold in quantity.

Maritime Zone: One of the five climatic zones in which grape growing areas are divided. This one is the coolest.

Medoc: Part of the Bordeaux Region. One of the great wine-grape growing regions of France.

Merlot: A red wine grape of considerable merit because it is usually blended with Cabernet Sauvignon to achieve the best red wines of Bordeaux. Now achieving some popularity as a varietal.

Méthode Champenoise: The original French method of making champagne wherein a second fermentation is induced in the bottle, with the carbon dioxide dissolved into the bottled wine.

Microclimate: A special set of growing conditions, usually confined to a small area. This could be induced by soil content, availability of water, or by geographical features of the site.

Mission grape: A heavy-bearing, somewhat sweet grape, probably of Mexican or Spanish origin, which was first planted in California by the early Franciscan Missionaries.

Moscato canelli: A very sweet white wine grape of the muscat family. It makes a luscious dessert wine.

Mosel: River in Germany and France, where it is called the Moselle. Also the wines grown in these regions.

Must: The pulped grapes, as they come out of the crusher and into the fermenting tank.

Noble grapes: Those varieties of grapes that yield the best wines, such as Cabernet, Sauvignon, Pinot Noir, Pinot Chardonnay. Usually they are hard to grow, yield sparsely, and like all good things, are achieved only with some difficulty.

Nose: The particular aromatic odor that is peculiar to any one wine.

Odium: A grape disease characterized by a powdery film of spores that attacks and mildews grapes.

Petite Sirrah: A red wine grape, originally from France, which is made into a varietal wine in the Napa Valley.

Phylloxera: A vine disease caused by a tiny underground louse that eats European rootstock.

Pinot Noir: A red wine grape, originally from Burgundy, which in the Southern Napa Valley yields an excellent varietal wine. Also, the wine made from this grape.

Pinot St. George: A red wine grape. Mostly grown in the hillside vineyards of the Napa Valley. Also the wine made from this grape.

Pomace: The residue remaining after wine has been pressed from the must.

Pressing: The process by which wine is extracted from fermented must. Done by squeezing the fermented, pulped grapes.

Racking: The drawing off of wine above the sediment. Done several times during the aging process to achieve maximum clarity.

Red wine: Wine produced from dark-skinned grapes, which impart their coloring to the final product.

Refractometer: An optical instrument that measures sugar content by means of optical refraction.

Rheingau: A major grape-producing area in Germany bordering on the river Rhine.

Rosé wine: A light red wine, produced by short contact with red grape skins.

Set: The fertilization of the grape flowers.

Suckers: Non-productive canes.

Tartrates: Salts of tartaric acid, that accumulate in an aging tank, and must be regularly removed.

Traminer: A white wine grape, originally from Alsace. In the Valley it yields a light, fruity, slightly sweet wine.

Varietals (wines): A wine named after the grape from which it is made.

Vinifera: A family of grapes whose characteristics lend themselves to making good wine. All Napa Valley grapes are of the Vinifera family.

Vintage dating: The classification of a wine according to the year in which it was fermented.

White Riesling: A white wine grape, originally of German origin, source of the popular Johannisberg Riesling wine. Also "Riesling," the wine made from that grape.

White wine: Wine produced from (usually) white or yellow grapes and fermented out of contact with the skins. Theoretically, white wine can be made from red grapes by fermenting it out of contact with the skins.

Wine: An alcoholic beverage made from the fermented juice of the grape. Beverages made from fruits, berries, etc., while they are undeniably alcoholic beverages are not, strictly speaking, wine.

Wine-thief: A hollow glass tube open at both ends. With one end plugged by a finger, after the tube has been inserted in the wine-barrel, it easily transfers wine from the barrel to the taster's glass.

Zinfandel: A red wine grape, or the wine made from it. Originally imported by Count Agoston Haraszthy.

PHOTO DATA

Professional photographers have long known there is no one camera always best suited for an assignment entailing a variety of situations. Selection of the photographic equipment used to do this book became a matter of compromise. The choice inevitably boiled down to the equipment which would do the best overall job, even though some other camera format could admittedly be better for any one specific picture. It was, therefore, almost inevitable that I should again turn to the 35mm cameras, since this equipment has demonstrated a versatility unmatched by any other format. The toughness, portability, wide variety of lenses and excellence of optics made the Nikon system a logical choice.

It is high tribute to the quality built into these Nikon instruments that in spite of the all-pervasive dust, moisture, sticky grape juice and the inevitable beating a camera in hard professional use gets, they are all in perfect working order today.

Four Nikon FTN bodies, and one Nikkormat were used to make the pictures in this book. Unless otherwise noted, all exposures were on Kodachrome II film, rated at ASA 25. Lenses used were all Nikkors, and unless otherwise noted, were capped with sky-light filters. Two flash units were used: a small pocket Ultrablitz and a 200 watt-second Matador with extension heads, a wonderfully versatile and powerful unit.

Page	Shutter Speed	Aperture	Lens	Notes
Cover	1/8	@ f 8	55mm	Macro, Weak fill-in flash
v	1/60	@ f 5.6	50mm	Fill-in flash
viii-ix	1/60	@ f 8	50mm	f 2
x	1/250	@ f 4	105mm	
xi	1/60	@ f 4	50mm	
xii-xiii	1/125	@ f 4	105mm	
xiv-xv	1/125	@ f 5.6	28mm	
xvi	1/250	@ f 5.6	50mm	
xvii	1/250	@ f 5.6	50mm	
xviii	1/8	@ f 16	28mm	Tripod
22	1/125	@ f 4	28mm	Pola-Screen
23	1/15	@ f 5.6	55mm	Macro, Tripod, Fill-in flash, six feet from cluster
24-25	1/4	@ f 5.6	300mm	Tripod
26	1/30	@ f 8	35mm	P.C.
27	1/60	@ f 5.6	50mm	f 2
28-29	1/4	@ f 16	28mm	Pola-Screen, Tripod
30	1/125	@ f 4	55mm	Macro
31	1/30	@ f 16	50mm	f 1.4
32	1/60	@ f 8	85mm	Fill-in flash
33	1/60	@ f 8	35mm	P.C. Pola-Screen, Kodachrome X
34	1/30	@ f 8	55mm	Macro
35	1/125	@ f 5.6	35mm	f 2
36	1/250	@ f 5.6	105mm	
37	1/30	@ f 4	85mm	
38	1 Sec.	@ f 4	105mm	Almost dark, Tripod
39	1/125	@ f 2	35mm	f 2
40-41	1/60	@ f 5.6	35mm	f 2
42	1/250	@ f 8	85mm	Kodachrome X
43	1/250	@ f 5.6	135mm	
44-45	1/250	@ f 8	35mm	f 2, Kodachrome X
46	1/250	@ f 5.6	35mm	f 2
47	1 Sec.	@ f 4	28mm	Kodachrome Type A, Tripod
48	1/8 Sec.	@ f 4	55mm	Macro, Very dark
49	1/60	@ f 5.6	35mm	f 2
50	1/60	@ f 5.6	85mm	Pola-Screen, Tripod
51	1/30	@ f 4	35mm	Cloudy and dark
52	1/125	@ f 8	50mm	f 1.4
53	1/15	@ f 5.6	105mm	Tripod
54	1/250	@ f 5.6	50mm	f 2

Page	Shutter Speed	Aperture	Lens	Notes
55	1/125	@ f 8	50mm	f 1.4
56-57	1/125	@ f 8	50mm	f 1.4
58	1/125	@ f 8	35mm	f 2, Kodachrome X
59	1/125	@ f 5.6	28mm	
60-61	1/15	@ f 8	20mm	Pola-Screen, Tripod
62	8 Sec.	@ f 4	28mm	Kodachrome Type A, Tripod
63	30 Sec.	@ f 4	28mm	Kodachrome Type A, Tripod
64	1/250	@ f 5.6	50mm	f 1.4
65	2 Min.	@ f 8	28mm	Kodachrome Type A, Tripod
66	1/15	@ f 1.4	50mm	f 1.4, Fluorescent filter
67	1/125	@ f 5.6	50mm	f 2
68	1/60	@ f 8	50mm	f 1.4
69	2 Min.	@ f 8	35mm	P.C., Kodachrome Type A, Tripod
70	1/125	@ f 5.6	35mm	f 2 (with insufficient flash)
71	1/250	@ f 5.6	50mm	f 1.4
72-73	45 Min.	@ f 11	20mm	Tripod, Kodachrome II was used for this long exposure.
74	1/250	@ f 4	105mm	
75	1/60	@ f 2.8	50mm	f 1.4
76-77	1/60	@ f 11	35mm	f 2
78	1/30	@ f 4	35mm	f 2.8
79	1/250	@ f 5.6	50mm	f 2
80	1/250	@ f 5.6	135mm	
81	1/60	@ f 8	85mm	Multiple (2) flash
82	1/15	@ f 2.8	35mm	f 2, Tripod, Kodachrome Type A
83	45 Sec.	@ f 8	28mm	Kodachrome Type A, Tripod
84	1/125	@ f 5.6	50mm	Early morning
85	1/8	@ f 4	28mm	Handheld!
86	1 Sec.	@ f 8	35mm	P.C. Fluorescent filter, Tripod
87	1/30	@ f 5.6	35mm	P.C. Pola-Screen
88-89	1/250	@ f 5.6	50mm	f 2
90	10 Sec.	@ f 5.6	28mm	Tripod, Kodachrome X, Candlelight
91	1/125	@ f 5.6	35mm	f 2, Pola-Screen
92-93	1/60	@ f 8	35mm	f 2 with 200 watt sec. flash fill
94	1 Sec.	@ f 11	200mm	Tripod
95	1/30	@ f 16	28mm	
96	15 Sec.	@ f 8	28mm	Fluorescent filter, Tripod
97	1/250	@ f 5.6	300mm	
98	1/60	@ f 5.6	28mm	Weak fill-in flash
99	10 Sec.	@ f 8	20mm	Tripod
100	1/60	@ f 4	35mm	f 2, Kodachrome X
101	15 Sec.	@ f 5.6	28mm	Tripod
102	1/125	@ f 5.6	50mm	f 2, Early morning
103	1/15	@ f 16	28mm	Tripod
104-105	1/125	@ f 5.6	50mm	f 2
106	1/15	@ f 2.8	50mm	f 1.4
107	1/60	@ f 8	50mm	f 1.4, Kodachrome X, Raining
108-109	1/15	@ f 11	55mm	Macro, Pola-Screen
110	1/15	@ f 5.6	105mm	Kodachrome A, Light source: modeling lamps from Honeywell Strobonars, Tripod.
111	1/60	@ f 5.6	28mm	
112	1/250	@ f 5.6	50mm	f 2
113	1/60	@ f 5.6	35mm	P.C., Tripod